The Making of a Preacher

5 Essentials for Ministers Today

Marvin A. McMickle

FOREWORD BY JAMES A. SANDERS

JUDSON PRESS
PUBLISHERS SINCE 1824
VALLEY FORGE, PA

The Making of a Preacher: 5 Essentials for Ministers Today
© 2018 by Judson Press, Valley Forge, PA 19482-0851
All rights reserved.

No part of this publication may be reproduced, stored in a retrieval system, or transmitted in any form or by any means, electronic, mechanical,
photocopying, recording, or otherwise, without the prior permission of
the copyright owner, except for brief quotations included in a review of
the book.

Judson Press has made every effort to trace the ownership of all quotes.
In the event of a question arising from the use of a quote, we regret any
error made and will be pleased to make the necessary correction in future
printings and editions of this book.

Except where otherwise indicated, Bible quotations in this volume are from
HOLY BIBLE, New International Version®, NIV®, copyright © 1973,
1978, 1984, 2011 by Biblica Inc. Used by permission. All rights reserved
worldwide. The New Revised Standard Version of the Bible, copyright ©
1989 by the Division of Christian Education of the National Council of the
Churches of Christ in the United States of America. Used by permission. All
rights reserved. And The Holy Bible, King James Version.

Interior design by Crystal Devine.
Cover design by Wendy Ronga, Hampton Design Group.

Library of Congress Cataloging-in-Publication data

Names: McMickle, Marvin Andrew, author.
Title: The making of a preacher / Marvin A. McMickle.
Description: Valley Forge, PA : Judson Press, [2018] | Includes
   bibliographical references.
Identifiers: LCCN 2018011443 (print) | LCCN 2018026395 (ebook) |
ISBN 9780817081911 (epub) | ISBN 9780817017996 (pbk. : alk. paper)
Subjects: LCSH: Pastoral theology.
Classification: LCC BV4011.3 (ebook) | LCC BV4011.3 .M435 2018
(print) | DDC
   251--dc23
LC record available at https://lccn.loc.gov/2018011443

Printed in the U.S.A.

First printing, 2018.

Also from Marvin A. McMickle and Judson Press

Preaching to the Black Middle Class: Words of Challenge,
Words of Hope

Living Water for Thirsty Souls: Unleashing the Power of
Exegetical Preaching

An Encyclopedia of African American Christian Heritage

Before We Say I Do: 7 Steps to a Healthy Marriage

Battling Prostate Cancer: Getting from
"Why Me" to "What Next"

The Star Book on Preaching

Profiles in Black: Phat Facts for Teens

The Audacity of Faith: Christian Leaders Reflect on the
Election of Barack Obama

Deacons in Today's Black Baptist Church

Caring Pastors, Caring People: Equipping Your Church for
Pastoral Care

Pulpit & Politics: Separation of Church and State in the
Black Church

Be My Witness: The Great Commission for Preachers

■ ■ ■

Other Books by Marvin A. McMickle

Where Have All the Prophets Gone? Reclaiming Prophetic
Preaching in America (Pilgrim Press)

A Time to Speak: How Black Pastors Can Respond to the
HIV/AIDS Pandemic (Pilgrim Press)

Shaping the Claim: Moving from Text to Sermon
(Fortress Press)

"Let Justice Roll: Progressive Voices for Social Justice" by PNBC
in partnership with *Our Daily Bread* published in 2017

Contents

Foreword

■ ■ ■

Rev. Dr. Marvin McMickle has been a long time writing this book, his seventeenth. I had the privilege of mentoring Marvin McMickle in the doctoral program at Union Theological Seminary in New York City until 1976 when he received a call to the pastorate of a church over in Montclair, New Jersey. At first, I was disappointed that he had chosen to abandon work on the doctorate in First Testament studies and instead go into the pastorate. God knows, I thought, we need African American professors in the field of Old Testament, but here this very promising young scholar has decided instead to go into church ministry. I felt at the time that he had perhaps opted-out.

But McMickle invited my Union Seminary colleague, James H. Cone, and myself to officiate at his installation as pastor of St. Paul's Baptist Church in Montclair. I accepted with some hesitancy but nonetheless went with Cone out to Montclair for the occasion. As the service got underway, I gradually saw that my student had not abandoned his work in academic excellence but had chosen to answer the call of his people at one of the the most crucial and critical times in the history of the American church and nation. The 1950s and '60s had seen the horrible lynchings of young activists for change in the South, as well as the assassinations of three young leaders, Martin Luther King Jr. and the Kennedy brothers, who had given their lives trying to make America the country it was supposed to be, and here McMickle was answering the call with the prophet Isaiah's response: "Here am I, send me." As Cone and I made our way back across the river to New York City, I realized what we had just borne witness to, but even so did not yet know how great the witness to divine righteousness and justice was by participating in the launch of McMickle's ministry in Montclair.

In this book McMickle draws on 35 years experience of pastoring churches in New Jersey and Ohio, plus four prior years of associate ministry in New York City while working on the doctorate, and now a full seven years serving as president of one of the leading seminaries in the country. His contributions in the fields of homiletics and church leadership include innumerable awards and honors, plus invited professorships at various universities and seminaries, including Yale University Divinity School and Princeton Theological Seminary. He knows whereof he speaks and writes. He knows the black church. He knows the white church. And he has spent a lifetime encouraging us all to be the witnesses to truth and justice we are called to be.

While this is McMickle's seventeenth published volume, some receiving prestigious awards, it is not just another book for McMickle. This one pulls together all those years of experience in an effort to challenge those who occupy pulpits around the country, and indeed the world, to speak truth to power in effective yet pastoral ways. In doing so, he takes the reader directly into the courts of Pharaoh Ramses the Great, the most powerful ruler in the world at the time, with the young Moses to relay the divine command to "let my people go." Firmly based on sound exegesis, McMickle's book takes the reader through the Exodus experience with the promise of a better government in a better land for a people enslaved, humiliated, and abused—but a people who did not always appreciate what their leader was doing for them. McMickle works not only through Exodus but shows the radical message of Jesus of Nazareth for a people similarly oppressed even in their own land by Roman imperialism, heavy taxation, and religious repression.

Right up front, McMickle focuses on what kind of person or character God calls on to witness to God's truth before a wayward people. He rightly notes that Moses was a murderer and a fugitive from justice when God spoke to him from a burning bush that wouldn't be consumed, an experience that turned Moses' life around figuratively and literally. It changed him from being a fugitive to being a called man of God, ready and eager finally to return to his oppressed people to represent them before the most powerful man on earth. McMickle then moves carefully through Moses' confrontation with Ramses, even the realization that God hardened Pharaoh's heart as Ramses contemplated, like the slave owners of the pre-bellum South, the great value cheap labor has for the economy of the privileged. McMickle realizes that if God had softened the heart of Pharaoh, the liberated Hebrews would have been obligated to Pharaoh for their emancipation, instead of to God.

In like manner, McMickle moves through the plagues Moses inflicted on the Egyptians to show how hard-hearted the wealthy can be when their riches are threatened. All this is followed by the way McMickle moves on then to show the deep-seated ingratitude the "saved" had when they later experienced some tough times on the way to Sinai and the Promised Land. McMickle makes it abundantly clear throughout the book how tough one has to be if one feels called to preach truth to power and yet also to minister to the called today.

Perhaps the most mind-expanding chapter is chapter 8, "Preaching in Context." McMickle himself has preached in so many different settings that he challenges current preachers to broaden their horizons and come to realize that a true witness to biblical truth cannot assume that she or he will be called on only to preach in familiar situations. McMickle's own first appointment was in the 1970s as associate pastor at the famous Abyssinian Baptist Church in Harlem while he was studying at Union Theological Seminary. While he saw back then that its witness in the Harlem community had changed since Adam Clayton Powell was pastor, it has changed even more dramatically since McMickle was on staff there.

McMickle goes on to recount how preaching in a Chinese American church was an even greater challenge since his sermon had to be translated simultaneously into Mandarin and Cantonese. He describes how he had to learn how to witness to Chinese Christianity on the fly in order to be effective—not to mention how the need to be translated on the spot breaks the normal rhythm he used when preaching in black churches. He tells us, "members of my congregation had joined me for the

The Making of a Preacher

service at the Chinese Christian Church of Cleveland, and all of us walked away with a new appreciation for the multicultural, multi-ethnic, and multilingual challenges of preaching." Mc-Mickle uses the experience to instruct up-and-coming preachers of a new era how to adapt preaching the gospel to strange even alien situations.

McMickle draws upon a variety of experiences of those who had gone before, including Socrates. He even quotes from "Peanuts" when Linus tells the hapless Charlie Brown that he's going to be a great prophet. Linus warns Charlie Brown that sometimes people won't listen to him because they often don't want to hear the truth; prophets speak the truth to powerful people, and power corrupts even good people. Why then, Charlie Brown wants to know, does Linus go ahead and speak to them? The answer Linus gives is that prophets are stubborn people. McMickles warns his readers that if the preacher preaches in order to hear nice words, she or he probably is not doing the work of a true prophetic witness to the gospel.

McMickle very clearly knows the history of the formation of the biblical text and how powerfully it spoke to the people in antiquity because he uses that knowledge to show his readers how radical the biblical challenge to comfortable people can be at any time in human history—and how comforting it can be to those who suffer because of the selfish ambitions of the power-ful. He draws on the history of the Ancient Near East to situate the power of the message of the prophets and of Jesus to the people in their time, and then how that very message can be as compelling in our situations today.

McMickle warns his readers not to be taken in by those who today claim they know the Bible but use it to advance an agenda based on a few passages that make up a scrapbook Bible, claim-ing it to be a "prophecy" that will benefit the few and turn "the other way" when the powerless suffer because of that message. He warns his readers not to be taken in by the Trump admin-istration's claims to be inspired by the Bible when those claims are in fact designed to assert their misguided interpretations of "Bible prophecy." He shows clearly how biblical prophecy is not prediction of what they claim is happening today, but on the contrary it is a sharp challenge to all such claims. He exposes the falsehood of citing Romans 13 to induce the faithful to accept authoritarian leadership by showing how faithful biblical prophecy exposes such falsehood. Romans 13:1-10 was cited by the Nazis in Germany to induce "good German Christians" to accept Hitler's authoritarian rule but they failed to go on and cite the rest of the Epistle to the Romans that put it all in context. The Prophets bravely and boldly challenged the authorities of their time as indeed did Jesus the Roman imperialism of his time.

This book should be read by every seminary student in the country, white or black, and it should be carefully parsed by those already in pulpits who need reassurance and help in continuing to do what they have been called to do. It will help empower their ministries and show how strong a guide the Bible critically read can be for true prophetic preaching in an age of Trump and all he stands for.

James A. Sanders, PhD
Professor Emeritus, Claremont School of Theology
and Claremont Graduate University
President Emeritus, Ancient Biblical Manuscript Center
Honorary Canon of the Diocese of Los Angeles

Acknowledgments

■ ■ ■

There is a beloved gospel hymn by Andraé Crouch that asks the question, *"How can I say thanks for the things you have done for me?"* The main focus of that song is giving thanks to God for the wonderful work of salvation through the death, burial, and resurrection of Jesus Christ. In this book for preachers about the task of preaching, I do give thanks to God for the miraculous ways in which my life has been changed from a rebellious youth roaming the streets on the South Side of Chicago, to a seminary president invited to pulpits, lecture halls, and convention platforms across the United States. *To God be the glory for the things he has done!*

I give thanks to all the preachers whose words and personal witness have had an impact on my life. I think about James T. Holland who was youth minister at Park Manor Christian Church in Chicago, and Charles H. Webb Sr. who was senior pastor of that congregation. In the absence of my own biological father who abandoned my family when I was ten years old, those two men were surrogate fathers and spiritual mentors for me. I think about Moses Crouse and Kenneth Mull of Aurora College, and also Asa Colby and J. Lloyd Dunham who anchored the Religion and Philosophy Department at that school. When I went on to begin graduate study in New York City in the 1970s, alongside classmates from Princeton and Harvard and Yale, I soon discovered there was nothing they had learned at those Ivy League schools that I had not also learned through those men in the ivy-covered walls of Eckhart Hall at Aurora College.

I give thanks to God for Lawrence N. Jones, James H. Cone, James A. Sanders, and the rest of the faculty at Union Theological Seminary in New York City. The dual emphases of that school were and continue to be the formation of scholarly pastors and pastoral scholars. It is impossible to describe how deeply those values were implanted in me and in my classmates at UTS. My commitment both to the local church and to the classroom of seminaries, to spiritual formation and to the active pursuit of social justice were birthed during my years at Union and Columbia University. I continue to draw fresh water from those wells almost fifty years later.

I give thanks for the preachers of New York City during the 1970s who set such a powerful example of pastoral leadership during my student years. I think especially of Samuel D. Proctor, William A. Jones Jr., Gardner C. Taylor, Sandy F. Ray, Wyatt Tee Walker, Edmund A. Steimle, and Ernest T. Campbell. Genesis 6:4 says, "In those days there were giants in the land" (KJV). The same could be said about many of the pulpits in New York City during the years I lived there: *giants were in the land.* The remarkable thing about that group of preachers was their open-door policy regarding Union students. All of them agreed to teach preaching courses at UTS. Those who were pastors invited Union students to preach in their churches. It was a rich and rigorous environment in which to hone the craft of preaching. I feel a sense of regret for any preacher who has not had the benefit of multiple mentors and role models not only as regards the art of preaching, but also as regards the art of civic and community engagement.

I owe a deep sense of gratitude to the congregations who had to sit through my sermons while I was learning how to preach at their expense. They listened freely. They chided and corrected gently. They affirmed my calling even when my gifting had not yet become apparent. Of course, there was one deacon at St. Paul Baptist Church in Montclair, New Jersey, who said to me one day: "When you first came to this church I wouldn't have given a nickel for your preaching." Even so, he kept coming to church every Sunday, perhaps in the hope that my preaching might be elevated at least to being worth a quarter! By the time I left St. Paul to begin a new ministry at Antioch Baptist Church in Cleveland, Ohio, well over two-hundred persons traveled from New Jersey to Ohio by car and by plane to share in my installation service. I can still hear Sheila Jackson from St. Paul saying to the people of Antioch, "We wanted to bring him to you with our love." How can I say thanks?

I am deeply grateful to Judson Press for its continued faith in me over the last eighteen years. Beginning with Randy Frame and Linda Peavy, and continuing with Rebecca Irwin-Diehl, Lisa Blair, Gale Tull, and Laura Alden, ours has been a partnership that I have cherished and valued. Writing a book is not a solo act. Preparing a full manuscript and sending it around in search of a publisher was not the way I wanted to proceed. Finding a publisher who can help to shape a book, provide rigorous editorial oversight, and force the writer to strive for maximum integrity as regards a single quotation or a single footnote is a crucial part of producing a book. It may be more difficult and take longer than self-publishing, but in my experience, it has proven to be a far better process that has yielded a far better product.

I am grateful to the Trustees and my faculty colleagues at Colgate Rochester Crozer Divinity School for allowing me to shape my role as a seminary president to continue in my role as an active teacher, researcher, and scholar. They have embraced my role as a writer, and they have also endured my constant urging that each of them does the same within their own fields of expertise. I am deeply committed to the notion that theological educators should function both as classroom teachers and as scholars whose books and articles are being read and considered by students and faculty at other schools. This is one of the lingering effects of my years at Union Theological Seminary.

A special word of thanks goes to James A. Sanders who read and critiqued each chapter of this book. He also agreed to write the Foreword. James H. Cone had begun to review these chapters as well, but his sickness and subsequent death did not allow him to finish this journey with me. James Cone was more than a teacher to me. He was the first African American scholar and writer I had ever encountered. He was only ten years older than I, but like so many other of his students, I wanted to emulate his example. What can you say about a man who single-handedly invented an academic field of study? Black theology sparked liberation theology, feminist theology, womanist theology, post-colonial theology, queer theology, and other lenses through which to reflect on Scripture and society.

Finally, I thank my wife, Peggy, for allowing me the time and space I need to prepare a book manuscript. Writing is an isolating process. Hours are spent on background reading, tracing sources in other books and journals, and deciding how to order and organize the massive amount of material that has been generated during the research phase. I have, sometimes, at the insistence of Judson Press editors, spent hours tracking down the accuracy of a single quote. The time it takes to do that is time I am not able to spend with Peggy. Sometimes she compensates for that by sitting with me in my study, reading while I work. More often, she goes to another part of the house and waits until I can take a break from the work. This is my seventeenth book, and she has followed this practice of support and encouragement every time. How can I say thanks?

Introduction

■ ■ ■

No one is born with the mindset, the disciplines, or the skills necessary to be an effective preacher of the gospel of Jesus Christ. Preachers are not born; they must be made. As with any profession or vocation, there may be a certain amount of innate talent or ability, but natural talent alone is not enough to sustain a person throughout a career in any field. In the book and the film *Hidden Figures*, it seems that Katherine Johnson, the black woman whose skills with mathematics and analytical geometry helped launch John Glenn into orbit around the earth, possessed some natural abilities that revealed themselves early in her life. Even so, she was sent to a school for gifted students where her natural abilities could be augmented and enhanced with formal instruction and a challenging curriculum.[1]

Some people possess natural talent for music, athletics, languages, automotive mechanics, or certain forms of technology. They are prodigies within those fields with skills and talents that amaze many who have practiced those crafts for a long time. Nevertheless, the road from being a prodigy to being a prolific professional at one's craft still requires years of practice, mentoring, intellectual formation, and testing one's self against the abilities of others in the same field. Wolfgang Amadeus Mozart was a child prodigy in the field of classical music, but his natural gifts were cultivated and enhanced by the supervision of his father, Leopold Mozart, who was himself a highly regarded musician. Athletes need coaching. Chefs need taste-testing. Authors need editors and critics. Actors need directors. Physicians and lawyers need professional associations to test their knowledge and hold them accountable in the performance of their work.

It is the same way with preaching. Individuals may possess certain natural gifts of speech or intellect. They may possess a certain ease in the public spotlight. They may even have a passion for worship and for the work of the church in the world. Persons who possess some or all of these traits might cause some well-meaning person in a congregation to announce that the one with such gifts should surely be a preacher. There is one thing that such persons forget, however: preachers are not born; they are made. No amount of natural gifts or talents is sufficient to make a preacher.

Preachers are made by stages of development over time. Preachers are made by trial and error in the use and development of their gifts. Preachers are made as they search for their own authentic voice and style, freeing themselves from becoming little more than clones of the persons who have had the most influence on their lives and on their ministry. Preachers are made by laying claim to their own perspectives on Scripture and theology which will guide and inform the content of their sermons and their ministry for decades to come. Preachers are made when they learn how to preach within the context of their time and place in history, heeding the advice of the German theologian Paul Tillich, who observed that "preaching must be done with an awareness of the present times."[2]

Preachers are made as they master the art introduced by the Swiss theologian Karl Barth, who said, "Preachers should have the Bible in one hand and a newspaper in the other."[3] While the printed text of the Bible is fixed and changeless, the newspaper and now all the twenty-four-hour news outlets of television and the Internet, not to mention the stream of social media, present us with an ever-changing array of circumstances. Those swiftly evolving current events make the content and usefulness of sermons preached in earlier decades largely irrelevant to the needs and questions of people in later generations. There is much to be learned about sermon style and structure from the masters of earlier generations such as

Jarena Lee or Charles Spurgeon or C. T. Walker. However, the application of their sermons may not speak to the challenges and curiosities of later generations of Christians. Sermons preached in Lee's eighteenth- and nineteenth-century Philadelphia, Spurgeon's nineteenth-century London, or Walker's early twentieth-century Augusta, Georgia, may have spoken powerfully to their own historical time and place. However, the "present time" that informed and shaped their preaching was dramatically different from the circumstances that define our postmodern age.

Preachers in the twenty-first century must learn how to function in a culture that is increasingly secular, social-media driven, nuclear-war threatened, politically partisan, and confronted with the claims of alternative facts and fake news. Preachers are made when they learn how to preach within and to their own time and place. No amount of natural talent can fully prepare a person for preaching under these circumstances. Preachers are made as they commit themselves to the disciplines of Bible study, curiosity about current events, and attentiveness to the rapid changes in how people today engage in religious life and practices.

Preachers are made as they move beyond the comfort and familiarity of preaching in their own pulpits on a Sunday morning and expand their ministry to include evangelistic events, denominational gatherings, clergy conferences, college and university chapels, civic gatherings, and public protests about unjust social policies and practices. Preachers are made when they move from a campfire at a youth summer camp, to a service for senior citizens in a nursing home, to a state prison where the congregation is comprised of both inmates and guards. Preachers are made as they engage in pulpit exchanges across racial, ethnic, denominational, and urban/suburban/rural communities. Preachers are made as they develop both the capacity and the comfort to preach before multiple audiences in multiple settings.

Some preachers may seem to have an early advantage, because they were born into a lineage of preachers. That was true for Gardner Taylor, William A. Jones Jr., or Martin

Luther King Jr. Each of them was part of a lineage of preachers that included their fathers and in some cases even their
grandfathers. The same could be said for Prathia Ann Hall,
H. Beecher Hicks Jr., Otis Moss III, or Jeremiah Wright Jr.
Each of them was the child of a widely known and highly
heralded preacher-parent or grandparent. There is no doubt
that when one grows up in a preacher's household such as
theirs there is a greater exposure not only to the preaching
of one's own parent but also to the constant stream of other
preachers from across the country that will likely appear in
the pulpit of their local church, but in their own homes as
well. Yet, each of those named above refused to lean solely
upon their pedigree as the child of a preacher. Instead, they
went through a process by which they themselves were further formed and shaped.

In his book about the preaching style and content of
Gardner Taylor, Jared Alcantara talks about the "apprenticeship" approach to learning how to preach that has been the
standard approach to preparing young preachers, specifically
within the African American church.[4] Alcantara notes that
"some of Taylor's mentoring relationships were woven into
his experience of growing up in the black church and were
thus a natural by-product of his being the son of a minister.
Other mentoring relationships he sought out first at Oberlin
and then in New York."[5] This process of learning how to
preach by listening to and being mentored by older and more
established preachers is referred to as "emulation" by Cleophus LaRue.[6] LaRue continues by saying, "To emulate is not
to copy but rather to set a standard of achievement by which
one gauges one's own preaching ability and advancement."[7]
Whether the term is apprenticeship or emulation or mentoring, the principle remains the same: preachers are not born;
they are made over time by many and varied processes.

The point being argued here is by no means limited to
African American preachers. There may be no more famous
parent-child preaching legacy in the history of the American
pulpit tradition than that of Lyman Beecher and Henry Ward
Beecher. The father, Lyman Beecher, is the one after whom the

prestigious Lyman Beecher Lectures at Yale Divinity School are named. The son, Henry Ward Beecher, delivered the first three lectures in that series, which began in 1872.[8] Henry Ward Beecher was often referred to as "the most famous man in America."[9] It was once observed that Lyman Beecher was "the father of more brains than any man in America."[10] That was largely because, in addition to Henry Ward Beecher, there was his sister, Harriet Beecher Stowe, who was the author of one of the best-known pieces of American literature: *Uncle Tom's Cabin*.

Despite the influence of his father, Henry Ward Beecher understood that preachers are not born fully prepared for that work. Preachers must be made over time, by experience and exposure, by spiritual formation and adapting to unanticipated physical challenges and setbacks, and by the guiding hand of mentors and the inward work of the Holy Spirit. Hence, he pursued formal training at Amherst College in Massachusetts and Lane Theological Seminary in Ohio.

I know scores of second-generation preachers following in the footsteps of at least one of their parents who are now serving in pulpits across the country. Some of them greatly exceed the fame and effectiveness of their preaching parent. Others of them never quite emerge from the towering shadow of their well-known and much-beloved preacher-parent. Either way, it might seem as if there is a built-in advantage to those for whom preaching is very nearly "the family business." I think of Rev. Edward Small, a colleague from Cleveland, Ohio, who had four sons, all of whom followed him into the preaching ministry. I also note Rev. Dr. Larry Macon, also of Cleveland, whose two sons now serve with him as associate pastors. There is no doubt that each of those second-generation preachers was greatly influenced by the example and perhaps even the urging of their preacher-parent. Nevertheless, preachers are not born; they are made.

Despite these examples of second-generation preachers, it is obvious that not every preacher, not even every *great* preacher, has a child who follows them into the preaching ministry. Being a preacher's child is in no way a predictor of the vocation those children will follow. I know of many instances when the children of preachers wanted to pursue very different career paths, but their preacher-parent pushed and shoved and urged their children to pursue a career in the preaching ministry instead. Occasionally things have worked out well when the call to ministry came not from heaven but from within one's own home. In other instances, the preacher who was "called" primarily by a parent eventually burns out, gives up, and turns to whatever vocation was their first and real passion.

Conversely, some of the greatest preachers of all time did not come from a lineage of preachers. Many of them were not even reared in the church. They were, instead, the ones God directed toward the preaching ministry, much to the amazement of almost everyone who knew that person before they expressed any interest in being a preacher. Not one of the first disciples of Jesus was on track to be a preacher. All of them were brought to that task after having already begun work in very different vocations. It is clear from Acts 9:10-19 that Ananias was not prepared for the message from Jesus that Saul of Tarsus, the great enemy of the church, was now about to become its chief spokesman throughout the Gentile world.

One of my colleagues in Rochester, New York, tells the story of an encounter he had when a childhood friend heard that my colleague was now a preacher. The friend told him, "You are not fit to be a preacher." My colleague responded by saying to his lifelong friend, "That's the same thing I told the Lord, but he called me anyhow." I can never forget a visit I received from an old girlfriend during my teenage years who, after some years of separation, had heard that I was now a preacher. She caught up with me at my father's funeral. She never knew my father, because my parents had divorced and he was largely out of my life long before I had met this girlfriend. However, she knew I would be there, and that would be her chance to confront me with this question: "I heard that you are now a preacher. How did you get from where we were then to where you say you are now? Because I know you!" All I could say to her was, "You knew me then, but you do not know me now. You do not know: 'What a wonderful change in my life has been wrought since Jesus came into my heart.'"

This brings us to the central question for this book: What steps are involved in the making of a preacher? It has been demonstrated that coming out of a distinguished lineage of preachers is not a necessary attribute for becoming a preacher. Possessing some of the outward gifts of a preacher is not enough to sustain a person in the preaching ministry. Coming out of a background that may seem to others as being antithetical to the message of the gospel or the example of Jesus does not disqualify a person from becoming a preacher. What, then, is involved in the making of a preacher? The chapters that follow will offer at least one approach to the process that will be called *The Making of a Preacher*.

A Five-Step Process

This book will set forth five steps that will serve as building blocks for the formation of a preacher. Using the life and work of Moses in the book of Exodus as a case study, this book will consider his ministry from the perspective of five distinct steps. Those five steps are hearing the call, confessing your character, claiming your content, knowing your context, and facing the consequences.

Hearing the Call

Call will be presented as the inward assurance that by whatever means or method, a person has become absolutely convinced that being a preacher is the work to which God has summoned them. Scripture seems to convey the idea that preaching is not a job for volunteers. Repeatedly the Bible points to people who expressed the conviction that by one means or another, God had called or commissioned them to the work of preaching. It is impossible to think about the preaching of Moses without first thinking about his encounter with God at the burning bush (Exodus 3:2-12).

Preaching should be viewed as a lifelong vocation. A person who has been called to preach may or may not always serve as the pastor of a local congregation. However, while people may retire from the pastorate or pursue their ministry in some other context, people who have been called to preach seldom if ever fully retire from preaching. As a result of their call, preaching is not simply what they do; preaching is who they are. They see sermon ideas coming at them from everywhere they look and from everything they see and hear. They anxiously await the next opportunity they have to mount the pulpit and say a word for the Lord. There may come a time when age and health will result in their no longer being able to preach, but even then, the impulse, the desire, the wistful yearning to preach one more time will always remain.

The call is more than the process by which persons first become aware of God's desire to use their lives in the ministry. The call is also the event that constantly reminds preachers of why they are involved in this work when moments occur throughout their ministry that leave them feeling defeated or depleted. Preachers soon find out that people do not conform to the teachings of the gospel simply because they heard our sermons. Preaching can often leave the preacher wondering if their ministry and their message are getting through, or if their heartfelt sermons are doing any good or bearing any fruit. There may come a moment when a preacher might want to throw up his or her hands and walk away. There are certainly less stressful ways to make a living. So why not just walk away? Perhaps it is because at their lowest moment they remember how it was and why it was they entered upon this journey in the first place. Maybe it is because they remember that this is the work to which God has called them. That will be the first step to be examined in the making of a preacher: the call of God upon their lives.

Confessing Your Character

Confessing (or testing) your character is the second step to be considered. Character will be presented as the quality of person the preacher is—before and after the call to preach. Who are the people whom God chooses to be preachers? From what backgrounds do they come? Were they saintly souls when God called them, or do they come from lives that might make them seem unlikely candidates for the sacred task of preaching the gospel? Is there an age range within which God always selects? Does God choose only from within a certain gender? Black suits and pulpit vestments tend to cover over a multitude of sins that have the capacity to haunt the memory of those of us who have been called to preach.

The people to whom we preach see only the finished product in the making of a preacher. What they usually do not see, and what they may never know unless the preacher reveals it, is who we were and how we lived before we acknowledged God's call on our lives. Preachers do not stand above or apart from the sins and entanglements that complicate the lives of those seated in the pews. When we stand to preach to them it is very much like the definition of preaching by D. T. Niles, who said, "Preaching is one beggar telling another beggar where to find bread."[11] Is anyone ready to preach unless and until they have done an assessment of their own character, their own past life, and their own sinful ways? Once preachers have held the mirror of God's mercy before their own faces they can truly say, "It ain't my mother or my father . . . It ain't my brother or my sister, but it's me, O Lord, standing in the need of prayer." Preachers are made when those who have been called to this work fully realize that our past sins, our sense of inadequacy, or our years spent running away from and even denying our call to ministry do not disqualify us from being used by God as preachers.

Confessing our character involves the prejudices, the biases, the quests for recognition and reward that we will have to struggle with, even try to preach through as we seek to be faithful to the God who has called us to be preachers. Character is best described by remembering the story of John Newton. At one point in his life he was an active profiteer in the trans-Atlantic slave trade that captured or purchased African people, sailed them across an ocean, and then sold them into lifelong slavery at auction blocks that stretched from Brazil to Barbados to Baltimore, often using ships built and owned by men in Boston. How is it possible that such a man could end up as an ordained Anglican priest who wrote "Amazing Grace," one of the most beloved of all Christian hymns?

Imagine that President Barack Obama sang a song written by a former slave trader at the funeral for a black preacher who, along with eight other members of Emanuel AME Church in Charleston, South Carolina, had been murdered by a white supremacist seeking to start a race war. How does this character shift occur? What was true for John Newton is true for most people, including most preachers: "I once was lost, but now am found; was blind, but now I see . . . 'twas grace that brought me safe thus far, and grace will lead me on."

Claiming Your Content

Claiming your content is the third step in the making of a preacher. Content involves those themes and topics which must be included in a preacher's schedule of sermons. There is a long list of harmless topics on which preachers can focus our attention. We can limit our preaching material and our text selection to be sure that as few people as possible are ever challenged or offended by our sermons, and so as many people as possible think well of us. However, there are only so many sermons on prosperity theology, or praise and worship, or the omnipotence of God that can be preached before people discover that the diet being fed to them from the pulpit is leaving them malnourished and ill-equipped to bring their faith to bear in the face of the hardships of daily life.

My former Old Testament professor, James A. Sanders, has recently written a book in which he acknowledges that he grew up in Memphis, Tennessee, during the Jim Crow era of racial segregation. He reports never having heard a sermon from the pulpit of his church that challenged or questioned what Sanders now refers to as "the American apartheid system."[12] He also reports on the resistance he began to feel from both friends and church leaders when he began to make justice issues a part of his preaching and teaching content. Preachers are made when they find the courage to speak about issues that are clearly present in the Bible but that are almost totally absent from the content of so many sermons being declared week after week after week.

Some preachers are more fixated on how they sound than they are on the substance of what they are saying. Sometimes the pursuit of eloquence trumps the hard work of biblical exegesis. Appealing to people's ears and emotions becomes more important than challenging them at the level of their hearts and consciences. In the audio recordings of his 1976 Lyman Beecher Lectures on Preaching, Gardner Taylor makes a point that sadly did not make it into the printed text of those lectures. He drew a sharp distinction between what he called "the manner" and the "matter."[13] The manner was how the preacher said certain things: tone, vocalization, alliteration and/or rhythm, and pacing. While such things are never to be ignored, the manner in which we preach is never an adequate substitute for the matter or the biblical and theological and current relevancy of our sermons.

Content involves matters of social justice. Content involves the staggering wealth disparity that has already taken root in this country. Content for twenty-first-century preachers must include matters of human sexuality, or the resegregation of American schools as a direct result of the continuing segregation found in so many American residential neighborhoods. Content involves the status of women and LGBT persons both within the broader society and within the life of churches and denominations.

Knowing Your Context

Knowing your context is the fourth step involved in the making of a preacher. As stated earlier, what is at issue here is where a preacher is willing to go to say a word of biblical content on behalf of the Lord. Do preachers limit themselves only to their own pulpit, their own local community, their own denomination, and their own racial or ideological group? Does a preacher refuse to go to city hall, not to preach a sermon but to testify on an issue of human rights or social justice? No matter how eloquent a preacher may be in expounding on Christian doctrine, there may come a time when their voice and eloquence will be needed to address the issue of fair housing at a meeting of the city council or to speak to a US Senator concerning that preacher's opposition to a US Supreme Court nominee whose confirmation might turn back the clock on hard-won human and civil rights gains.

Preaching is needed at summer camps where children and teens gather around a campfire. Preaching is needed in prisons where inmates and guards are confined together in overcrowded and sometimes inhumane conditions. Preaching is needed in senior citizen facilities and nursing homes where people are no longer able to travel to church on their day of worship. Preaching is needed on college and university campuses where issues of faith may not otherwise be discussed. Preachers are made when they are willing to carry their ministry beyond the comfortable and familiar confines of their own church, and, like the prophet Jonah, go to places they initially may want to avoid.

However, context is far more than one's physical location while preaching. Context is also one's awareness of the times during which one is preaching. O. Wesley Allen's book, *Preaching in the Era of Trump*, is an example of context informing content. That book seeks to challenge preachers to focus the attention of preachers on "the potential for significant harm that his [Trump's] presidency could do to the ethical fabric of our society."[14] Context involves preaching during the Black Lives Matter movement. Context involves preaching in the aftermath of the rally in Charlottesville, Virginia, where white nationalists and neo-Nazis waved swastikas and Confederate battle flags, and where an automobile driven by a hate-filled driver smashed into a crowd and killed a young woman.

Context involves preaching during a time when people with enormous power to shape national policy are climate change deniers who reject the scientific evidence of how human behavior contributes to global warming. In light of that, context involves preaching while one deadly hurricane after another rips through the Caribbean, Florida, Louisiana, and Texas. It is stunning to hear the head of the Environmental Protection Agency try to explain the strength and recurrence of these killer storms without making any reference to global warming. It is equally shocking to hear the Secretary of Education for the United States speak about improving school safety in this country while refusing to talk about gun violence which has reached epidemic proportion in our nation's schools. Preachers are made as they find ways to address the social, political, and cultural issues present in the world around them.

Facing the Consequences

Facing the consequences is the fifth step in the making of a preacher, and it is inseparably linked to the earlier references about character and content and context. There may be some people who will reject what preachers say because they refuse to hear such a message coming from that person. Some people may not want to hear a message about such themes as women in ministry, racial injustice, LGBTQI concerns, sermons about the rights of Palestinians in their dealings with the state of Israel, or issues that intrude too much into partisan political issues. Often, resistance to and rejection of certain topics can be anticipated. The question then arises as to whether or not the preacher proceeds to say what Scripture teaches and what God demands, even if it is met with unpleasant consequences within the congregation, the community, or the denominational structure within which that preacher operates.

Sometimes you do not know what consequences you may encounter until after you have said or done something. I recall a memorial service that was held after the mass shooting at Sandy Hook Elementary School on December 14, 2012, during which persons of all faith traditions stood and prayed together. However, when Rob Morris, a pastor from Newtown, Connecticut, who served within the Lutheran Church Missouri Synod participated in that service, he was later forced to offer an apology to his national church body for going against that denomination's policy that "prohibits joint worship with people of other faiths."[15] Years prior, a Missouri Lutheran pastor, David H. Benke, was suspended from his ministry in Brooklyn, New York, for appearing at a separate 9/11 memorial service.[16]

Everything we say and do as preachers will not always result in universal applause and approval. Preachers are made as they pass through times of testing to discover whether they will preach not only in season, when their words are well-received, but also out of season, when what they say might carry negative consequences for themselves and their ministry.

Is there a topic that a preacher will not discuss because he or she is afraid of the consequences? Is there a justice issue they will not support because they are afraid of the consequences? Is there a person of great power and influence whose words or deeds a preacher will not challenge or critique because they are afraid of the consequences? A preaching ministry can be greatly limited if a preacher spends time with every sermon worrying about who might be offended by the words or even the broad themes of his or her sermons. I do not take this matter lightly. I am not ignoring how a preacher might have to pay a price for preaching what is not widely and broadly popular and acceptable within the church or the surrounding community. All I am suggesting is that part of the making of a preacher involves wrestling with the predictable and sometimes the unexpected consequences of what is said in a sermon.

Methodology for This Book

In terms of the methodology for this book, the five principles set forth above will be considered through the lens of a single biblical character, Moses. This book will look at the call experience of Moses at the burning bush (Exodus 3:2-6). It will consider the character of Moses as someone who was a fugitive from Egyptian justice when it was discovered that he had committed murder (Exodus 2:11-15). It will focus on the core message of Moses which has become the basis of all expressions of liberation theology: "I have observed the misery of my people who are in Egypt; I have heard their cry on account of their taskmasters" (Exodus 3:7). It will look at the issue of context when God says to Moses, "So come, I will send you to Pharaoh to bring my people, the Israelites, out of Egypt" (Exodus 3:10). Finally, it will look at all the consequences Moses faced when Pharaoh told him, "Get away from me! Take care that you do not see my face again, for on the day you see my face you shall die" (Exodus 10:28).

As the story of Moses is unfolded, readers will be invited to consider their own journey of faith. As they work their way through these five steps, and as they are forced to think about their own preaching ministry through the lens of these five building blocks, they will better understand what is required to be an effective preacher of the gospel. Preachers are not born; they must be made. This five-step process is one way to think about *The Making of a Preacher*.

▪ ▪ ▪

Notes

1. *Hidden Figures*, Twentieth Century Fox, 2016.
2. Paul Tillich, quoted in *The Preaching of the Gospel* by Karl Barth (Philadelphia: Westminster Press, 1963), 54.
3. A version of this quote appears in an interview with Karl Barth (*Time*, May 31, 1963). For extended comments, see The Center for Barth Studies, Princeton Theological Seminary, http://barth.ptsem.edu/about-cbs/faq.
4. Jared E. Alcantara, *Learning from a Legend: What Gardner C. Taylor Can Teach Us about Preaching* (Eugene, OR: Cascade Books, 2016), Kindle edition, location 1517.
5. Ibid.
6. Cleophus J. LaRue, *I Believe I'll Testify: The Art of African American Preaching* (Louisville, KY: Westminster/John Knox Press, 2011), 28.
7. Ibid.
8. Edward DeWitt Jones, *The Royalty of the Pulpit* (New York: Harper and Brothers, 1951), 3–4.
9. Debby Applegate, *The Most Famous Man in America: The Biography of Henry Ward Beecher* (New York: Three Leaves Press, Doubleday, 2006).
10. Ibid., 12.
11. D. T. Niles, in *20 Centuries of Great Preaching Volume Twelve*, edited by Clyde E. Fant, Jr. and William M. Pinson, Jr. (Waco, Texas: Word Books, 1971), 174.
12. James A. Sanders, *The Re-birth of a Born-Again Christian* (Eugene, OR: Cascade Books, 2017), 6.
13. Gardner C. Taylor, *How Shall They Preach: The Lyman Beecher Lectures and Five Lenten Sermons* (Elgin, IL: Progressive Baptist Publishing House, 1977). This quote was on the audio recordings but does not appear in print in these lectures.

14. O. Wesley Allen, *Preaching in the Era of Trump* (St. Louis, MO: Chalice Press, 2017), 5.

15. Marc Santora, "After Rebuke, an Apology for Pastor in Newtown," *The New York Times*, February 12, 2013, https://www.nytimes.com/2013/02/13/nyregion/rev-matthew-c-harrison-offers-apology-for-his-rebuke-of-newtown-pastor.html.

16. The Associated Press, "Lutheran Panel Reinstates Pastor After Post-9/11 Interfaith Services," May 13, 2003, https://www.nytimes.com/2003/05/13/nyregion/lutheran-panel-reinstates-pastor-after-post-9-11-interfaith-service.html.

Chapter 1

The Call to Ministry

There the angel of the LORD appeared to him in flames of fire out of a bush. Moses saw that though the bush was on fire it did not burn up. So Moses thought, "I will go over and see this strange sight—why the bush does not burn up." When the LORD saw that he had gone over to look, God called to him from within the bush, "Moses! Moses!" —Exodus 3:2-4, NIV

■ ■ ■

It is my firm conviction that those who are engaged in the ministry of preaching the gospel of Jesus Christ should do so only if they are responding to a clear sense that this is the work to which they have been called by God. Preaching the gospel—declaring the timeless story of salvation through faith in Christ—may not be the best choice for persons who say to themselves, "This is the work I want to pursue," whether or not they sense some urging or leading from God. The famous story of Isaiah 6:1-8 may seem to contradict this claim. It may seem, based solely upon verse 8, that Isaiah was volunteering to be used by God. Nothing could be further from the truth when the whole passage is considered. Isaiah was not someone who volunteered for God's service. Rather, he was someone who was already a temple priest in Jerusalem, and thus was already in a ministry position when he expressed his willingness to be reassigned. More importantly, his willingness to answer God's call to service came only after he had experienced one of the most dramatic manifestations of God's presence recorded anywhere in Scripture. It came after his own confession of unworthiness to be a servant of God. Finally, it came after an angel had touched his mouth with a burning coal, purging him and preparing him for the service to come. In a sense, the question from God and the answer from Isaiah must be read and considered only in light of the dramatic actions that preceded them.

Consider also the most-noted instance of a person who is trying to volunteer to become a disciple of Jesus, that being a teacher of the law (Matthew 8:19). Jesus sent him away with a warning about the hardships associated with being one of his followers. This is relevant for anyone who is engaged in Christian ministry. There will inevitably be times of disappointment, disillusionment, and even despair as the best of our preaching seems to fall upon rocky ground. Clergy burnout is a constant reality. The one thing that may allow persons to remain in the ministry when they feel like giving up is their deep sense of being called by God to this work. If there is no sense of being called, then the warning of Jesus in Matthew 8:20 will likely be the result.

Everyone, from the prophets of the eighth, seventh, and sixth centuries BCE, to all the disciples and apostles of Jesus in the New Testament, engaged in the ministry of preaching in response to being called and equipped by God for that work. This was true for the Old Testament prophets who accounted for their preaching by saying, "The spirit of the Lord is upon me." This was also true for all the disciples and apostles of the New Testament who responded to the challenge from Jesus first to "follow me, and I will send you out to fish for people" (Matthew 4:19, NIV). That was followed by the so-called Great Commission in which Jesus told those same men, "Therefore go and make disciples of all nations" (Matthew 28:19-20, NIV; the quote is from verse 19).

It is impossible to talk about the ministry of Saul of Tarsus without reflecting on his dramatic encounter with Jesus on the road to Damascus as recorded in Acts 9:3-6. That experience resulted in his sudden transformation from an avowed enemy of the church who was set on a mission to destroy the message about Jesus, to his eventually becoming the apostle Paul who would be the preeminent preacher of the message of Jesus to the Gentile world and the attributed author of nearly one-half the books of the New Testament. As dramatic as his encounter with Jesus was, the most important part of that experience was in verse 6, when Saul is told, "Now get up and go into the city, and you will be told what you must do" (NIV). Saul was not responding to the emotion of the moment on the Damascus Road. He was responding to the message that he would be told what he should do in preparation for the work that God was going to assign to him.

Even Jesus himself accounted for his ministry by invoking the notion of being called by God. In Luke 4:18-19, when he returns to the synagogue in his hometown of Nazareth he reads these words from the scroll of Isaiah: "The Spirit of the Lord is upon me, because he has anointed me to bring good news to the poor. He has sent me to proclaim release to the captives and recovery of sight to the blind, to let the oppressed go free, to proclaim the year of the Lord's favor." Then, as if to further clarify his meaning, he says in verse 21, "Today this scripture has been fulfilled in your hearing."

This notion of Jesus being called or sent or set aside for the work of God is reinforced in John 3:16-17 (NIV): "For God so loved the world that he gave his one and only Son, so that whoever believes in him shall not perish but have eternal life. For God did not send his Son into the world to condemn the world, but to save the world through him." The operative words are "God gave" and "God sent." In John 12:27, when Jesus was wrestling with the prospects of what awaited him in Jerusalem after his triumphal entry, he made the following observation about the ministry to which he had been called: "Now my soul is troubled. And what should I say—'Father, save me from this hour?' No, it is for this reason that I have come to this hour." Thus, it was not only the prophets and apostles who functioned under a clear call to ministry; it was also Jesus himself who accounted for his work and his words by stating that this was the work assigned to him by God.

This brings us back to the central claim of this book, which is that preachers are not born; they are made. The first step in being made into a preacher is being called by God to that ministry. Some might want to point to the prophet Jeremiah: "Before I formed you in the womb I knew you, and before you were born I set you apart; I appointed you as a prophet to the nations" (Jeremiah 1:5, NIV). Of course, the issue with Jeremiah was not that he was born to be a prophet, but that even before he was born God had "set him apart" and "appointed him" to be a prophet. As with all the other prophets and apostles in Scripture, Jeremiah's ministry was the result of being called to that task by God. Moreover, in Jeremiah 1:9-10 (NIV) it says, "Then the LORD reached out his hand and touched my mouth and said to me, 'I have put my words in your mouth. See, today I appoint you over nations and kingdoms.'"

This story is matched by that of Isaiah, whose call was confirmed after God touched his lips with a burning hot coal and then sent him out to preach (Isaiah 6:6-9). Ezekiel was told by God, "I am sending you to the Israelites . . . you must speak my words to them" (Ezekiel 2:3-7, NIV). Amos reports, "I was neither a prophet nor the son of a prophet, but I was a shepherd, and I also took care of sycamore-fig trees. But the LORD took me from tending the flock and said to me, 'Go, prophesy to my people Israel'" (Amos 7:14-15, NIV). Many of the other biblical prophets (Micah, Joel, Jonah, Obadiah, Habakkuk, Zephaniah, Haggai, Zechariah, Malachi, and Hosea) also allude to their experience of being called by God simply by saying, "The word of the LORD came to me."

While one preacher's call story may not be as dramatic as that of another, there should be some moment, some movement of the Spirit that allows the preacher to say in the words of the hymn, "I know the Lord has laid his hands on me." The making of the preacher begins in earnest with the call of the preacher.

How Do You Know You Have Been Called?

Writing in *God's Yes Was Louder Than My No*, William Myers reflects on the call stories of several preachers he had interviewed. In each case, they spoke about something that

Myers calls "the urge," which is an inner conviction, perhaps not yet fully matured, that God was at work in their lives leading them to the preaching ministry. Odell Jones, who was interviewed by Myers, spoke about the urge as "an inner dissatisfaction with doing anything else except the ministry."[1] Caesar Clark, one of the best-known and most-beloved preachers of an earlier generation, also spoke about this urge in a similar fashion. Clark stated, "You do not preach because you want to; you preach because you cannot help yourself . . . So you have that inner urge, it haunts you, and you only have a sense—a feeling—of satisfaction when you yield to it."[2]

God Struck Me Dead is a collection of slave narratives from the nineteenth century. It offers a series of dramatic reports of how preachers, even while still living under the yoke of slavery, were called to the preaching ministry. One of those narratives involves a man who described his call as "being hooked in the heart."[3] It was almost as if he imagined that God was fishing for a preacher and this man was the one whom God pulled up.

You get a sense of this in the lives of both Jeremiah and Paul. In Jeremiah 20:9 (NIV), that prophet declares, "If I say, 'I will not mention his word or speak any more in his name,' his word is in my heart like a fire, a fire shut up in my bones. I am weary of holding it in; indeed, I cannot." Similarly, Paul says in 1 Corinthians 9:16 (NIV), "For when I preach the gospel, I cannot boast, since I am compelled to preach. Woe to me if I do not preach the gospel!"

There is another indicator that many who have felt the urge to preach have later used as a validation of their being called by God to that ministry. Myers refers to Dr. E. L. Harris, who said, "If a man can keep from preaching he ought not to preach, because if he can keep from preaching, that is a sign that he hadn't been called to preach."[4] In my own case, any number of persons, both clergy and laity, said to me, "If you can be happy and content doing anything else except being a preacher, then you should do whatever that other thing is that brings you satisfaction." Preachers are made as they come to understand, instantly or over time, that this is the work to which they have been called, for which they have a compelling urge or fire, and which is the only vocation that brings them peace and contentment.

I am familiar with the notion that the local church often plays a role in helping persons discern a call to ministry. Of course, the church confirms a call to ministry through acts such as ordination and eventual placement into places of service. However, there may be instances in which the church recognizes gifts of ministry in a person even before the person in question is fully aware of them. Even in those instances, one is left to wonder whether such an approach is effective if it is not eventually accompanied by some conviction discerned through prayer and personal reflection that it is God, and not just well-meaning members of a congregation, who is calling that person into ministry.

This combination of a clear sense of being called to the ministry and the role that is played by the church in confirming that call was in full display in the call experience of one of the most widely known African American preachers of the twentieth century, Joseph Harrison Jackson. Best known for his role as president of the National Baptist Convention, USA, Inc., from 1953 to 1982, it is less known that his ministry began in 1908 at the age of eight when he was granted a preaching license by the New Hope Baptist Church of Cohoma County, Mississippi. In writing about that call experience, Sherman Tribble writes:

> Jackson stated that there had been no earth-shaking or cataclysmic experience that guided him to ministry. Instead, he felt that he had always been called to preach. The church shared the sentiment that his witness was credible and thereby granted him a preaching license. Even though he had no educational experience, he did have a Christian experience, an encounter with the Divine. Moreover, he had a call from God which the community validated as being evident in his spoken witness.[5]

What about Clergy Burnout?

I want to be careful in separating the call to preach from the common experience of clergy burnout. There are a great many preachers whose calling was clear and certain but who have since left the ministry. That increasing reality should not be viewed as making their call invalid. It should rather be viewed as a stark realization that preaching, especially in the context of pastoral ministry, is a demanding vocation that creates strains that are physical and emotional and that have an effect not only on the preacher but on that preacher's family as well.

All congregations have people who place unusual demands on the pastor in terms of time and attention. Such demands can become more than some faithful pastors can bear. In fact, it could be argued that many more preachers might well have left the ministry were it not for the fact that they were sustained and bolstered by the certainty that this was the work to which they have been called by God. In 2010, *The New York Times* reported that other factors contribute to the rate of clergy burnout; most notably that some clergy, in response to the demands of their congregation, have willingly become workaholics who seldom if ever take any time off for themselves and their families. In addition, fewer and fewer congregations can afford to support a full-time clergy person. That results in the necessity of more and more preachers becoming bi-vocational just to support themselves and their families.[6] That article resulted in an ongoing online discussion among clergy in 2015 led by Tod Bolsinger under the heading, "The True Cause of Pastoral Burnout."[7]

Thus, it is becoming increasingly true that many persons who were called to the ministry and served as preachers and pastors for many years are now leaving the profession in record numbers. As a single example, the United Presbyterian Church reported that in 2005 there was a quadrupling in the number of people leaving the profession during the first five years of ministry, compared with the 1970s.[8] I want to speak sympathetically about clergy burnout, and I do not in any way want to suggest or imply that a preacher's decision to leave the ministry is in any way related to their call having been invalid or uncertain! Not everyone who leaves the ministry does so because they have not been called. They may do so because of sickness, financial stresses, family problems, unexpected career opportunities outside of the ministry, or the time demands that pastoral ministry often imposes upon persons. What is being argued here is that burnout will likely be experienced much earlier in their ministry by those who are not conscious of and are not reenergized by the abiding and unshakable assurance that this is the work to which they have been called by God.

The Call of Moses

Now that there has been a general discussion about the matter of being called to preach, we move, as promised, into a discussion about the call of Moses. There may be no more compelling call story in the entire Bible than the call story of Moses found in Exodus 3:1-10.

> Moses was keeping the flock of his father-in-law Jethro, the priest of Midian; he led his flock beyond the wilderness, and came to Horeb, the mountain of God. There the angel of the LORD appeared to him in a flame of fire out of a bush; he looked, and the bush was blazing, yet it was not consumed. Then Moses said, "I must turn aside and look at this great sight, and see why the bush is not burned up." When the LORD saw that he had turned aside to see, God called to him out of the bush, "Moses, Moses!" And he said, "Here I am." Then he said, "Come no closer! Remove the sandals from your feet, for the place on which you are standing is holy ground." He said further, "I am the God of your father, the God of Abraham, the God of Isaac, and the God of Jacob." And Moses hid his face, for he was afraid to look at God.
>
> Then the LORD said, "I have observed the misery of my people who are in Egypt; I have heard their cry on account of their taskmasters. Indeed, I know their sufferings, and I have come down to deliver them from the Egyptians, and

to bring them up out of that land to a good and broad land, a land flowing with milk and honey, to the country of the Canaanites, the Hittites, the Amorites, the Perizzites, the Hivites, and the Jebusites. The cry of the Israelites has now come to me; I have also seen how the Egyptians oppress them. So come, I will send you to Pharaoh to bring my people, the Israelites, out of Egypt."

A preacher's call to ministry may not be as dramatic as that of Moses with a burning bush that is not consumed and by the unmistakable voice of God. In fact, as R. Alan Cole points out in his commentary on Exodus, "The true revelation was not the burning thorn bush, but God's word that came to Moses there."[9] The call may or may not result in an immediate response by the preacher. However, in more instances than not the call does take the form of being redirected from a path that a person has already chosen for themselves and being redirected to a path that had never before crossed their mind. Moses did not wake up that morning with any thoughts about returning to Egypt, or standing before Pharaoh, or leading the Hebrew people out of bondage. He woke up that morning wondering where he would find water and grazing for his sheep. However, by the time he went to bed that night both his vocation and his direction had been completely altered. Moses was beginning the process of being made into a preacher.

Walter Brueggemann adds much to our understanding of the call of Moses, and the difference between *how* God got the attention of Moses and *why* God sought to get the attention of Moses. Brueggemann writes:

The theophany [appearance of God] happens in two parts. The better-known part of the appearance is the burning bush . . . The second part of the encounter is the speech of God. There is the sovereign summons. God calls Moses in a double summons. Moses' response, following convention, is "Here am I," indicating readiness to submit and obey. This exchange establishes the right relation of sovereign

and servant. This is the first hint we have that the life of Moses has a theological dimension, for the categories of his existence until now have been political.[10]

Moses' story is instructive for preachers today for several reasons, each one of which we will explore in turn:

- God calls the preacher by name.
- The preacher responds to God's call.
- The call is not only *to* something but also *from* something.
- The call is no respecter of age.
- The call may require relocation.

God Called Moses by Name

There are several things about this description of the call of Moses that shed light on how the call should be experienced by everyone who feels themselves drawn to the preaching ministry. First, the issue is not the presence or absence of any dramatic events that attend one's calling. The burning bush caused Moses to turn aside in curiosity; it got his attention (vv. 2-3). God was not casting around to see who in that region might be interested and available. God called Moses by his name (v. 4).

R. Alan Cole reinforces this point about the personal nature of being called when he says, "The whole concept of Christian calling derives from the belief that God has communicated with us personally, and has called us by name."[11] The first key insight in Moses' story is the realization that by one means or another, God has summoned you, individually and personally, to be a preacher.

Moses Answered God's Call

According to Brueggemann, who draws upon the work of John Calvin, the second thing of interest regarding the call of Moses comes when Moses says, "'Here am I,' indicating readiness to submit and obey."[12] The call is not simply God summoning us to divine service. The call awaits our response.

There may be some preachers reading this book who knew God had called them to be a preacher, but it took them a great many years before they agreed to "submit and obey." I preached the ordination sermon for a dear friend of mine whose call by God was apparent to everyone who knew him but which he himself took years to acknowledge.

Granted, Moses became a bit more hesitant and reluctant about his call when he realized it would require him to return to Egypt and stand in the presence of Pharaoh (see vv. 11-22). Nevertheless, what eventually sent him on that journey back home to Egypt was the realization that the God of Abraham, Isaac, and Jacob had called him by name, and he eventually submitted to that assignment.

"Called to" Involves Being "Called from"

The third thing to point out regarding the call of Moses is that he was called from one vocation to another. Moses was not idle and unoccupied when he saw the burning bush and heard the voice of God and was charged to become God's messenger. Moses had settled into the life of a nomadic shepherd. He had been tending the flock of his father-in-law, Jethro, for many years. That was the reason he was close enough to Mount Horeb to see the burning bush; he was going about his duties as a shepherd.

Like the prophet Amos, who described himself by saying "I was a shepherd, and I also took care of sycamore-fig trees" (Amos 7:14, NIV), Moses was an agricultural worker taking care of the sheep that were essential to nomadic people whose food, clothing, housing, religious rituals, and financial security depended upon the size and health of their sheep and goats. Moses was not simply being called to go to Egypt with a message of liberation for the Hebrew people. Moses was also being called to leave behind the vocation in which he was already engaged. Moses was not called from vacation to vocation; he was called from one vocation to another.

As with Amos and Moses, God often calls the preacher into a new vocation that requires that person to leave a former life behind. This call from one profession to another was also at work when Jesus called James and John to leave behind their established jobs as fishermen and to "fish for people" instead (Matthew 4:19, NIV). Similarly, the apostle Matthew was challenged to leave behind his profitable job as a tax collector and follow Jesus (Matthew 10:3). Most famous of all the New Testament characters called into the ministry of the gospel of Jesus Christ is the apostle Paul, who was a well-established Pharisee and a vocal opponent of Jesus, who would later be called and would become the primary messenger of the gospel to the Gentiles (Acts 9:1-6).

This is a reminder that not everyone who is called into the ministry comes right out of college or has the ministry as their first vocation. An increasing number of persons are like Moses, Amos, James and John, Matthew, and Paul; preaching is their second career. The same could be said about Deborah, Huldah, Priscilla, Phoebe, and other women who were called to various forms of service and leadership in both the Old Testament and New Testament.

In my preaching classes over the years, I have encountered male and female students who were former or retired physicians and dentists, engineers, school teachers, career military personnel, entertainers and artists of one type or another, and even former professional athletes. I have even had persons who came to my classroom by way of a prison cell after serving time for having formerly been robbers, or drug dealers, or pimps or prostitutes. The point is, Moses is a reminder that the call to preach can come and literally call us from one vocation to another.

What about Age?

The fourth thing to note with the call story of Moses involves the matter of age.[13] While the call story of Moses in Exodus 3 does not make any explicit reference to his age at the time, there is broad agreement that Moses was a man of advanced years when God called him into service. Exodus 7:7 says that Moses was eighty years old and Aaron eighty-three when they spoke to Pharaoh. The message for us in the twenty-first century is that we are never too old to be called by the Lord and used in God's service. While most people who are called into the ministry will likely have that experience at an earlier age than was the case for Moses, it should not surprise anyone when God calls people who are approaching or have already passed retirement age. Moses is a reminder that there is no such thing as being too old to be called by God.

That was certainly the case when the call of God came to Abram and Sarai in Genesis 12:1-4. Abram was seventy-five years old and Sarai (being ten years younger) was sixty-five when God called them to leave their home. They were eighty-six and seventy-six years old, respectively, when Ishmael was born (Genesis 16:16). When God changed their names to Abraham and Sarah, he was ninety-nine and she was eighty-nine (Genesis 17:1). And Abraham was one hundred years old and Sarah was ninety when Isaac was born (Genesis 21:5). Clearly, advanced age is no guarantee that God will not call someone into service.

Of course, as Paul cautioned his young protégé Timothy, there is also no such thing as being too young: "Don't let anyone look down on you because you are young" (1 Timothy 4:12, NIV). I know of a great many people whose call came and whose ministry began at a very early age in life.

The Challenge to Change
The fifth matter to consider involves the challenge not just to change one's vocation but also to change one's physical location. The call of Moses involved God sending Moses to an assignment in Egypt, hundreds of miles and a hot and hostile desert away. God was not calling Moses to assume a task within the radius of his present location. He was, like Abraham in Genesis 12:1, being asked to leave his country and obey God's call to move. There are those in ministry who are part of a system in which bishops can and often do move pastors from one location to another, often as frequently as every three to five years. However, accepting membership within those denominations assumes both an awareness of and an acceptance of that eventuality.

For others, like my brother and sister Baptists, changing our physical location is usually viewed as a matter of personal choice, not divine prerogative. The question is whether the acceptance of the call to preach is not simply a matter of vocation but also an openness to go or to be sent to places by divine direction whether that location matches our preferred career path or not. The call story of Moses seems to be an answer to that question. When God calls us, God is seeking our faithful response both to a change in our vocation but also to the location in which our ministry is to occur.

I can remember sitting in a student lounge in McGiffert Hall at Union Theological Seminary in New York City a few days before our graduation in 1973. The conversation shifted from reflections on our years together as students, to what we hoped or dreamed might be the next chapter in our lives. The range of career hopes was interesting, as everyone seemed to know exactly what they wanted to do next, as well as knowing exactly where they wanted to do it. Some dreamed of teaching at Harvard or Yale or even coming back to Union. Others spoke about pastoring large congregations in Texas or California or New York City. For most of us involved in that discussion, we had resolved the issues of vocation and location for ourselves. Who needed to hear from God; we knew exactly what we wanted to do next.

Then someone spoke up who temporarily put all of us to shame. That person said, "I will go wherever the Lord leads me." That was a humbling moment for those of us who had just told God what our plans were. I say that he temporarily put us to shame, because while we thought he had completed his statement, he had really only paused. He then went on to say, "So long as it is no farther west than Pittsburgh and no farther south than Baltimore." Suddenly, he was as prescriptive about his plans as the rest of us: "I will go anywhere the Lord leads, so long as it is no farther west than Pittsburgh, and no farther south than Baltimore." Given that we were currently sitting in New York City, that person was not giving God much room within which to operate. What the call story of Moses reminds us of is the fact that the obedience and submission that Brueggemann associated with the call of Moses includes obedience and submission so far as matters of vocation and location are concerned.

Barbara Brown Taylor offers some helpful insights into the call from God. She says in her book *The Preaching Life*, "There are calls to faith and calls to ordination, but in between there are calls to particular communities and calls to particular tasks within them—calls into and out of relationships as well as calls to seek God wherever God may be found."[14] Renita Weems offers further insights into the idea of being called when she observes: "One of the things about asking about your call is 'called to what?' I think the presence of women in the ministry forces the church, forces us, forces our colleagues to have to rethink the notion that in the black church only the preaching ministry is the ordained ministry in our churches."[15] Her point is well-taken; not everyone who is called to ministry is necessarily called to preach. Even Paul acknowledges that in 1 Corinthians 12:28 when he says, "God has appointed in the church first of all apostles, second prophets, third teachers; then deeds of power [miracles], then gifts of healing, forms of assistance, forms of leadership, and various kinds of tongues." Paul instructs us by saying in verse 11 that "all these things are activated by one and the same Spirit, who allots to each one individually just as the Spirit chooses."

Two of the most formative influencers of my life and ministry were the theologian James Cone and the Old Testament scholar James Sanders. Neither one of them saw their ministry as being defined by preaching, but who could ever doubt that both of them were called by God to teach! Evangelists like Billy Graham and Tom Skinner were called to preach but not to be pastors of local churches. I never dreamed that my certain call to preach the gospel would lead to a thirty-year career as a seminary professor and now as a seminary president. This one thing is certain: once God calls us into ministry, there is no guarantee regarding our particular communities or our particular tasks. The only certainty that will follow us wherever our career path may lead is that it was God who called us by whatever means or method, and it was each one of us who responded to God, as Moses did, by saying, "Here am I." All of this is part of the making of a preacher.

■ ■ ■

Notes

1. William H. Myers, *God's Yes Was Louder Than My No* (Grand Rapids, MI: Eerdmans, 1994), 27.
2. Ibid.
3. Clifton H. Johnson and Paul Radin, *God Struck Me Dead* (Philadelphia: Pilgrim Press, 1969), 19.
4. Myers, *God's Yes*, 27.
5. Sherman Roosevelt Tribble, *Images of a Preacher: A Study of the Reverend Joseph Harrison Jackson* (Nashville: Townsend Press, 1990), 5.
6. Paul Vitello, "Taking a Break from the Lord's Work," August 2, 2010, *The New York Times*, http://comment-news.com/story/d3d3Lm55dG-ltZXMuY29tLzIwMTAvMDgvMDIvbnlyZWdpb24vMDJidXb-3V0Lmh0bWw. Barna's 2017 State of Pastors report suggests that clergy are doing better in this area (see https://www.barna.com/burnout-breakdown-barnas-risk-metric-pastors/).
7. Tod Bolsinger, "The True Cause of Pastoral Burnout," ChurchLeaders.com, February 4, 2015. The conversation is ongoing. See also Claudio and Pamela Consuegra, "My bucket is running empty: Cumulative stress in ministry," *Ministry Magazine* (July 2018), 10–13.
8. Vitello, "Taking a Break."
9. R. Alan Cole, *Exodus*, Tyndale Old Testament Commentaries (Downers Grove, IL: InterVarsity Press, 2008), 71.
10. Walter Brueggemann, "Exodus," *The New Interpreter's Bible* (Nashville: Abingdon, 1994), 712.
11. Cole, 71.
12. Brueggemann, 712.
13. The matters of race, gender, and orientation will be considered in subsequent chapters.
14. Barbara Brown Taylor, *The Preaching Life* (Cambridge, MA: Cowley Publications, 1993), 23.
15. Renita Weems, quoted in William Myers, "Disentangling the Call to Preach: Certainty, Ambiguity, Mystery," in *Sharing Heaven's Music: The Heart of Christian Preaching—Essays in Honor of James Earl Massey* Barry L. Callen, ed. (Nashville: Abingdon, 1995), 47.

Chapter 2

Reflection on My Own Call Experience

> But Moses said to God, "Who am I that I should go to Pharaoh, and bring the Israelites out of Egypt?" He said, "I will be with you; and this shall be the sign for you that it is I who sent you: when you have brought the people out of Egypt, you shall worship God on this mountain." —Exodus 3:11-12

■ ■ ■

I must confess that my insistence that a preacher must be called to that vocation is largely informed by the Scriptures explored in the previous chapter and from the anecdotes I shared from other preachers. However, I would be unfaithful to the central claim of this section about the call if I did not acknowledge that my insistence on the idea of preachers being called is also informed by my personal experience with God. If there is one thing of which I am certain, it is that God called me into the ministry and made me into a preacher. The events surrounding my call story remain vivid more than fifty years after they occurred.

The Story of a Pink Candle in 1964

I had gone to a Christian summer camp outside of Chicago in 1964. My reason for going to camp had nothing to do with the pursuit of a religious vocation. All my friends at my local church in Chicago, including some very attractive girls, were going to camp that week. Thus, friendship and infatuation were the reasons why I went to that camp site.

The camp program extended from Sunday afternoon until the following Saturday morning. Every day was filled with crafts, sports, great meals, and community-building activities. Every evening featured a worship service around a campfire led by a local pastor who volunteered to spend that week with us at the camp. I have absolutely no recollection of what happened around that campfire from Sunday through Thursday evening. Not one word that was spoken that entire time had any lingering impact on me. However, what happened on Friday night changed my life forever.

I do not remember the sermon that the pastor preached, but I will always remember what happened after the sermon was over. He said that any of us who wanted to commit ourselves to being faithful followers of Jesus should go to a table he had set up on one side of the campfire and take a white candle. He then told us to put that candle under our pillow that night, pray a prayer of dedication to be a faithful Christian, and take the candle home the next day as a reminder of our decision.

Then he continued by saying that anyone who felt that they were being called to or wanted to learn more about entering some Christian vocation like being a pastor or a missionary should go to a table on the other side of the campfire and take a pink candle. Those who chose a pink candle were told not only to put the candle under their pillow and pray about their decision but also to report their sense of calling to ministry to the pastor of their home church, who could then begin to guide and mentor them in next steps.

To this day, I am absolutely sure that I went to the table where the white candles were sitting. Even though it was a half-hearted commitment, I at least agreed to try to live as a faithful Christian. That was about as far as my interests extended at that time. I took that white candle back to the cabin where I was assigned. I placed it under my pillow, but I did not offer any prayer or give any further thought to what it represented. I just went to sleep. The next morning, we were to pack up our belongings, head off to breakfast, and then board the buses to return home. I packed up my clothes and toiletries, and then turned to get my pillow and sleeping bag. When I lifted the pillow, there was a pink candle laying there.

I *know* that I did not go to the table where the pink candles were sitting. I *know* the candle I took from the table I went to was white. It was white when I picked it up, and it was white on Friday night when I placed it under my pillow. The next morning, however, the candle was *pink*.

I began looking around the cabin to see if anyone was looking at me with a smirk or a guilty grin on their face that might be a giveaway that they had switched my candle during the night. But no one was paying me any attention. On the bus ride home, I became more assertive and asked who it was that had switched my candle from white to pink. No one had any idea what I was talking about. My best friend at the time was the son of our pastor, and since he was on that bus coming back from camp, he urged me to share this story with his father.

Upon doing so, the pastor was sufficiently impressed by these events that he announced to the congregation that "Marvin has had a call to ministry from the Lord." Even that announcement, which was heard by all the young people of the church who had attended camp with me, did not result in anyone coming forth to confess that they had or knew who had switched that candle.

Martin Luther King Jr. and the Summer of 1966

I confess that the experience with the pink candle was not sufficient to move me toward a Christian vocation. It was gripping and mysterious, but it was not decisive. I went on with my life as a high school student. I attended Chicago Vocational High School, where I studied graphic design and the operation of linotype printing presses. After I graduated I was hired by Poole Brothers Printing Company to operate linotype machines. I was thrilled when I discovered that Poole Brothers Printing Company was at that time the sole producer of *Playboy* magazine, which was headquartered in Chicago. Part of my duties involved the production of some of the print portions of that magazine. By the standards of 2018 and online pornography, *Playboy* is tame, but in 1966 it was quite risqué, so much so that the stores that carried the magazine would display it so that only the word *Playboy* but not the full cover of the issue could be seen. Here I was as a seventeen-year-old boy printing *Playboy* magazine, managing on a regular basis to go two floors upstairs where the pictures were being printed. It was clear that the pink candle was having no effect on me up to that time.

Things changed dramatically while I was having lunch one afternoon inside the print shop. I was reading one of the Chicago newspapers and noticed that Dr. Martin Luther King Jr. was coming to Chicago to begin an open housing campaign. At that time, Chicago was rated as the most segregated city in America in terms of neighborhood housing patterns. The point of this summer-long civil rights campaign was to demonstrate that racism and segregation were not problems localized in the states of the former Confederacy in the southern United States. In fact, those problems were nationwide, especially where housing patterns were concerned. I had heard and read about Dr. King for years but never dreamed that he would be coming to my city for anything more than a one-night speaking engagement. This was to be a summer-long campaign, much like the ones previously held in Birmingham and Selma and other southern cities. Only, this one was going to be in my hometown of Chicago.

The opening rally for that summer campaign was to be at Liberty Baptist Church, right on the bus line that I used to come and go from my job every day. I decided that on the day of the first rally I would get off that bus at 46th and South Parkway and go inside Liberty Baptist Church to hear Dr. King for myself. I did not know it then, but God was continuing the process that had started with that pink candle. God was making me into a preacher.

Dr. King entered the church to thunderous applause. He was shorter than I had imagined he would be, so I could not see him as he made his way down a side aisle of the church because the people had risen to their feet. He eventually reached the rostrum and was now in full view. After the choir sang a few selections, he gave his remarks, which concluded with him inviting us to come to a city-wide rally at Soldier's Field in downtown Chicago that upcoming Sunday afternoon.

I and several of the young people from my church, all of us without the knowledge or permission of our parents, went to that rally. More than forty thousand people were there. Dr. King delivered a stirring address, and Mahalia Jackson, who lived in Chicago, sang several of her most-beloved gospel songs. That rally was followed by weeks of demonstrations that involved mass marches into some of the most racially segregated neighborhoods in the city of Chicago. I was present for several of those marches. I saw the swastikas being held up by so-called white Nazis. I heard the awful racial slurs such as "niggers go back to Africa." I also saw Dr. King leading those marches, unflinching even though he was personally the object of so much of the venom that was being spewed. I saw a model of what it meant to be a preacher that I had never seen before. This was not a pastor content to preach a safe message to a friendly and familiar congregation. This was someone who was laying his life on the line every day to speak truth to power.

Aurora College (1966–1970)

The pink candle from 1964 and the experiences with Dr. King in 1966 were beginning to work together to make me into a preacher. However, that work was far from finished. I left my job at Poole Brothers Printing Company, convinced that whatever God had in store for me, it no longer involved working in the production of *Playboy* magazine. I enrolled at Aurora College, about seventy-five miles west of Chicago. As fate would have it, my first course there as a pre-ministry student was in New Testament. The course was taught by Wayne Barton, an able New Testament scholar with a PhD in New Testament Greek from New Orleans Baptist Theological Seminary. When he entered the classroom two things struck me right away. First, he was wearing an open-collared shirt that revealed his bright "redneck." Second, when he opened his mouth his thick Louisiana accent came booming through. I was just one month removed from being involved in civil rights marches with hate-filled white people shouting and throwing everything imaginable at us, including bottles filled with urine and rocks big enough to crack our skulls. All of that was going on while the Chicago Police Department seemed far more interested in harassing us than in stopping those who were threatening our lives. And now my first class in college was with an instructor who in sight and sound embodied the spirit of the Old South.

I immediately shut down. I was unable to look at or listen to that man. He had not done anything to me or said anything that I found objectionable in terms of New Testament interpretation. Rather, he had unleashed in me my own racial prejudice rooted in recent experience that prevented me from judging him as an individual. I was doing to him what so many whites had done to black people for so long: despise a person because of their color. I received a failing grade in that class, because I did not do any of the work required to get a passing grade. It was the only F I ever received in my entire academic career from elementary school through graduate school. I retook that course one year later with a man from Minnesota named Kenneth Mull, who had earned his PhD at Northwestern University in Evanston, Illinois. The content of the course was no different from the course with Wayne Barton. The only difference was that Kenneth Mull did not remind me of the people I had seen and heard during our marches through neighborhoods in Chicago. I went on to earn an A in that course.

How could I possibly have known that three years later, Wayne Barton would offer me a job as a chaplain's assistant at The Illinois Correctional School for Boys in St. Charles, Illinois, where he was the head Protestant chaplain? How could I have known that for three consecutive summers during my break from studies at Union Theological Seminary in New York City, I would be invited to live in the home of Wayne Barton and his wife, Christine? The man I had despised because of his color and culture ended up being one of my best friends.

I remember writing an exegesis paper a few years later at Union for James A. Sanders in which I looked at Luke 16:19-22, the story of the rich man and Lazarus. My conclusion was that the rich man was the moral equivalent of white people in America, oppressive and insensitive to the sufferings going on around them. Conversely, I presented Lazarus as the moral equivalent of black people, finally redeemed by God from the hardships they had endured. I read the text through the lens of my personal experiences influenced by racism.

I was, perhaps, unconsciously reflecting views I had picked up from reading *The Fire Next Time* by James Baldwin. In that book, Baldwin was giving voice to his response after meeting with Elijah Muhammad, leader of the Nation of Islam, who asserted that all white people are demonic. Baldwin said:

> **That sinners have always, for American Negroes, been white is a truth we needn't labor, and every American Negro, therefore, risks having the gates of paranoia close on him. In a society that is entirely hostile, and, by its nature, seems determined to cut you down--that has cut down so many in the past and cuts down so many every day—it begins to be almost impossible to distinguish a real from a fancied injury. . . . Most Negroes cannot risk assuming that the humanity of white people is more real to them than their color. And this leads, imperceptibly but inevitably, to a state of mind in which, having long ago learned to expect the worst, one finds it very easy to believe the worst.**[1]

For a great many years, I was living with the paranoia expressed in that exegesis paper: all white people were flawed when it came to their dealings with any black person.

My paranoia was abruptly challenged when my paper was returned. Dr. Sanders wrote these words across the top of the cover sheet: "Whenever you read a biblical text and come away feeling better about yourself, you can be sure that you just misread that text." I was being challenged to understand that I could not be a faithful preacher of the gospel of Jesus Christ if I was predisposed to judge all white people by their appearance or regional accent, as opposed to their individual character. I could not challenge the racial prejudices of white people while I was at the same time exhibiting the same traits myself. I had to learn that the words of Dr. King had to apply as much to white people like Wayne Barton as they did to me: "I have a dream that one day my four little children will live in a world where they will not be judged by the color of their skin, but by the content of their character."[2]

Through a series of such events I now realize that while God may have called me to preach, I was not yet ready to be entrusted with the job. As with other areas of my life, this spiritual transformation did not come quickly. There were other lessons I had to learn, other people I had to encounter, and other things about myself I had to face honestly. What I understand in retrospect is that preachers are not born; they are made. As early as my first encounter with Wayne Barton in 1966, God was beginning to make me a preacher.

Union Theological Seminary (1970–1973)

In fact, it would take another full decade (spanning 1966 to 1976) before most of what God intended to do in my spiritual formation was complete. From 1970 to 1973, while at Union Theological Seminary in New York City, I was especially influenced by two professors, James Cone, who taught systematic theology and was just establishing the field of black theology, and James Sanders, who taught Old Testament and was just establishing the field of canonical criticism as a way of doing biblical interpretation. This fusion of black theology with its focus on God's identification with the Hebrew people being held in slavery in Egypt and an even deeper study of how the Old Testament reveals a God who always identifies with the poorest and the powerless provided a theological and theoretical foundation for my preaching that has informed me for the last forty years.

While studying in New York City I was exposed to the most remarkable assembly of preachers one could imagine. Nearby in the borough of Brooklyn, William Augustus Jones Jr. was at Bethany Baptist Church, Gardner Taylor was at

Concord Baptist Church, and Sandy F. Ray was at Cornerstone Baptist Church. Next door to my residence hall at Union Seminary was Riverside Church, where Ernest Campbell was the preaching minister, and where preaching greats from around the world made regular appearances. Also in Manhattan at Canaan Baptist Church was Wyatt Tee Walker, former chief of staff of the Southern Christian Leadership Conference under Dr. King. There was also Adam Clayton Powell Jr. at Abyssinian Baptist Church in Harlem. How could I know when I arrived in New York City in 1970 that two years later I would be invited to work at that great and historic church?

My primary preaching professor at Union was Edmund Steimle, a Lutheran preacher who had been for many years a regular voice on the NBC National Radio Pulpit. Thanks to him, a rich variety of great preachers appeared in James Chapel at Union Seminary. Without ever leaving New York City, I was able to hear and, in many cases, meet and come to know some of the most widely respected preachers in the United States. God was making me into a preacher, both in terms of the content of my sermons (what was I saying) and the rich array of preaching styles and sermon structures to which I was being exposed (how I was saying it).

Abyssinian Baptist Church (1972–1976)

There is no doubt in my mind, however, that the single greatest contributor to my being made into a preacher was being hired to work on the ministerial staff of the Abyssinian Baptist Church of New York City and to work with its new senior pastor, Dr. Samuel DeWitt Proctor. From 1937 to 1972 the pastor of that church had been Adam Clayton Powell Jr. He had succeeded his father, Adam Clayton Powell Sr., who had been senior pastor from 1908 to 1937. Thus, for sixty-four years that church, which had grown to a membership of fourteen thousand persons, had been led by that father-and-son team. The father was one of the leading figures of the National Baptist Convention.[3] The son became one of the leading political figures in the history of the United States, as well as an early leader in the nonviolent, direct-action phase of the civil rights movement.[4]

The church needed a pastor of national reputation, but not necessarily one that would continue the denominational legacy of Powell Sr. or the political legacy of Powell Jr. Samuel Proctor proved to be that person. As president of two historically black colleges (Virginia Union University and North Carolina A&T University), head of a division of the Peace Corps under President John Kennedy, a ranking executive with the Council of Economic Opportunity under President Lyndon Johnson, and a distinguished academician, Dr. Proctor brought instant stability, administrative leadership, and powerful preaching to that church.

Of equal importance to me was that he also hired three young preachers who would share in the pastoral work of the congregation. Dr. Proctor came to Abyssinian while retaining his endowed chair at Rutgers University as Martin Luther King Jr. Professor of Education. To fulfill all the duties of the pastoral role, he took half of his salary and had it designated as salary for the three preachers who worked alongside of him. Along with William S. Epps and Calvin O. Butts III, I was one of those three young preachers. My first paid position in the ministry was at a church that in 1972 had a membership of six thousand persons with a sanctuary that seated twenty-five hundred.

In a real sense, four years of practical experience at Abyssinian were as invaluable to my growth and development as three years of academic training at Union. I watched as Dr. Proctor presided at church board and congregational meetings. I saw him envision, coordinate, and successfully complete major fundraising efforts. I was often dispatched to a New York City airport to pick up guest preachers that ranged from Benjamin Mays of Atlanta, to Kelly Miller Smith of Nashville, Leon Sullivan of Philadelphia, Jesse Jackson of Chicago, and non-clergy speakers like Vernon Jordan and A. Philip Randolph.

I heard Dr. Proctor preach sermons that weaved current events, his own rich and rigorous practice of reading, the informality of his Southern upbringing, and his absolute intolerance for racism or bigotry of any kind. Amazingly, I was frequently entrusted with the responsibility of Sunday morning preaching in that church, as well as performing baptisms and presiding at the Communion table. I was ordained by that church in 1973, and I was married in that church in 1975.

One of the great thrills of my life came in 2010, when I was called upon to preside at the wedding of my own son, Aaron, and his wife, Pilar, at Abyssinian. We stood in the same spot where my wife, Peggy, and I had stood thirty-five years earlier. Whatever success I have had in ministry over the last forty years is directly the result of the mentoring that I received at Abyssinian during the four years between 1972 and 1976. I was being made into a preacher.

We Are the Totality of Our Experiences

It is very likely that most people who feel themselves called into ministry, and especially into the preaching ministry, will not point to one single place or one single person that or whom can completely account for the person they have become. As Barbara Brown Taylor has said, "We are called to particular communities—and to particular tasks within them."[5] My call involved a pink candle in 1964—encountering Martin Luther King Jr. in Chicago in 1966—struggling with my own racist response to Wayne Barton during my college years of 1966 to 1970—being stretched and challenged by James Cone and James Sanders at Union Theological Seminary from 1970 to 1973—being dazzled by the preaching of William Augustus Jones Jr., Gardner Taylor, and Sandy F. Ray in Brooklyn from 1970 to 1972—and being mentored and molded by Samuel Proctor from 1972 to 1976.

It is important for me to state that my call to ministry involved those persons who already held a PhD degree: Cone, Sanders, and Proctor, all of whom challenged me to follow suit. It involved the political activism of Adam Clayton Powell Jr., whose presence occupied every inch of Abyssinian Baptist Church years after his death in 1972. Even though I never met him, it was Powell's example that sparked my own lifelong interest in politics and public office.

My being made into a preacher can be traced to other roots and other sources as well. It involved the music of Motown that filled my ears with its steadily increasing socially conscious messages. It included the militancy of Malcolm X passed on to me in my teenage years by the Black Muslim barbers in my neighborhood barber shop in Chicago who cut my hair every two weeks and were always trying to recruit me into the Nation of Islam. It involved my mother, who was the first true book lover I ever knew and who passed that love of books on to me.

It involved Rev. Charles H. Webb Sr., who was my pastor at Park Manor Christian Church in Chicago, who drove me and his son, Charles Jr., across the country to national church conventions. It involved Rev. Mary G. Evans, pastor of Cosmopolitan Community Church, who was our family pastor during my early years of life. She was the first preaching voice I ever heard. She is the reason why I dismiss out of hand any notion held by some of my male colleagues even to this day that women cannot and should not preach. She was a far better preacher than any of the male preachers I ever heard speak disparagingly about women in the ministry and in the pulpit.

My First Call to Be a Pastor (1976–1986)

I was called to be the pastor of St. Paul Baptist Church of Montclair, New Jersey, in September 1976, at the age of twenty-seven. Not surprisingly, I was brought to the attention of that church by Dr. Samuel Proctor when they turned to him for a recommendation of someone to be their next pastor. I was twelve years removed from the pink candle. I was ten years removed from Poole Brothers Printing Co. and my summer with Dr. King. In truth, the Spirit never stops working on those God calls to be a preacher. I still see God's hand at work smoothing off my rough edges, filling out my spiritual life of prayer and study, and revealing to me what it is that I am being called to do—and to do next. However, I am certain of this one thing: from 1964 to 1976 the God who had called me at sixteen years of age and who was sending me to my first pastoral assignment at twenty-seven years of age had been making me into a preacher.

▪ ▪ ▪

Notes

1. James Baldwin, *The Fire Next Time* (New York: Dell, 1963), 93–94.
2. Martin Luther King Jr., quoted in James M. Washington, ed., *A Testament of Hope: The Essential Writings and Speeches of Martin Luther King Jr.* (New York: Harper and Row, 1986), 219.
3. Marvin A. McMickle, *An Encyclopedia of African American Christian Heritage* (Valley Forge, PA: Judson Press, 2002), 76–78.
4. Ibid., 129–31.
5. Barbara Brown Taylor, *The Preaching Life* (Cambridge, MA: Cowley Publications, 1993), 23.

Chapter 3

A Question of Character

One day, after Moses had grown up, he went out to where his
own people were and watched them at their hard labor. He saw
an Egyptian beating a Hebrew, one of his own people. Looking
this way and that and seeing no one, he killed the Egyptian and
hid him in the sand. . . . When Pharaoh heard of this, he tried
to kill Moses, but Moses fled from Pharaoh and went to live in
Midian. —Exodus 2:11-12,15 (NIV)

■ ■ ■

This chapter will focus on the character of those whom
God calls to preach. This focus on character does not
suggest anything about the strengths or admirable
qualities that a preacher might or must possess, and
about which he or she might be deservedly proud. Instead, I
am inviting preachers to take a long and hard look at several
other questions and concerns. First, what kind of person were
you when or before God called you to preach? It is likely
that all of us, like Moses who serves as the point of reference
throughout this book, have something in our background
that might in the eyes of the churches we now serve disqualify
us from serving in the ministry.

After all, Moses was a murderer and a fugitive from Egyptian justice (Exodus 2:11-15). The sole reason why Moses
was in the land of Midian was not because he decided to
relocate there of his own volition. He fled there, he went into
hiding there because he understood that his murder of an
Egyptian who was beating a Hebrew slave had come to the
attention of Pharaoh himself: "When Pharaoh heard of it, he
sought to kill Moses" (Exodus 2:15).

What does it say about the character of the people that denominational leaders and local church search committees might be searching for, when we consider that God called Moses into service even though Moses had committed murder? If God called Moses, sinful past and all, then whom are we willing to consider for admission to the ministry? Are there any character traits or sins of the past that can and should serve as an automatic disqualifier from any form of Christian ministry? Should the pulpit be reserved only for perfect people who never have to struggle with the sins of their past?

Does God only call people who fit into the twenty-first-century description of what constitutes "Christian values"? Or is God free to call former drug dealers into the ministry? Can God make use of people who had formerly been involved in the sex industry either of pornography or prostitution or pimping other people for personal profit? Can God use people who have spent some time in prison? If God could take a slave trader like John Newton and cause him to write the words for the song "Amazing Grace," then who is beyond the reach of God for service in the ministry? In short, did God call us into ministry because of or despite who we were and what we might have previously done?

God Calls People the Church Might Have Rejected

I think about Jeb Stuart Magruder, who worked in the White House during the presidency of Richard Nixon. He got caught up in the Watergate scandal, pled guilty to conspiracy, cooperated with federal prosecutors, and in exchange for his testimony about his role in that scandal served only seven months in a federal prison. That much is well known by people who followed the events of the Watergate episode between 1971 and the decision by Richard Nixon in 1974 to resign from the office of President of the United States.

What may be less known is the course of Magruder's life upon his release from prison in 1975. He wrote a book entitled *From Power to Peace* about his deepening Christian faith.[1] In that book, he stated what happened to him that resulted in his imprisonment. He said, "Somewhere between my ambition and my ideals I lost my ethical compass."[2] As a way to restore that compass he enrolled in Princeton Theological Seminary, where he and I were students at the same time. He was a master of divinity student there from 1978 to 1981, while I was working on a doctor of ministry from 1980 to 1983.

Given the recent nature of the Watergate scandal, less than ten years earlier, almost every person on that campus had lived through those events and knew exactly what Magruder had said and done. It should not be surprising, therefore, that many people on the Princeton campus at that time wondered aloud about what to make of the presence of Jeb Stuart Magruder. Was a former defender of a disgraced American president a suitable candidate for the ministry of Jesus Christ? Was his presence at Princeton a charade, a cover-up of a past that he was trying to escape? Was he seeking to use the ministry as a hiding place, just as many persons a decade earlier had rushed into seminary not because they had been called into the ministry but because they used attendance at a divinity school as a way to avoid being drafted into the US military and sent off to fight in Vietnam?

Charles Colson, another person sentenced to prison for his involvement in the Watergate scandal, also became actively involved in a church-based program known as Prison Ministry Fellowship following his release from federal prison. The difference seemed to be that unlike Magruder, Colson did not claim a call to the ministry. He did not enroll in seminary. He seemed to focus his work on helping incarcerated persons make a new start in life upon their release. Churches across the country got involved in a program called Project Angel Tree that provided Christmas gifts and a Christmas party for the children of persons who were going to be incarcerated during the Christmas season. That program was started by Charles Colson and sponsored by Prison Ministry Fellowship. One could account for what Colson was doing by pointing to Matthew 25:31-44, where Jesus lists the care for the prisoners as one of the characteristics of all faithful Christians.

It seemed to many people that what Jeb Stuart Magruder was doing was something quite different. He was not simply taking to heart the forms of Christian love and concern for "the least of these" that God expects from every believer. Magruder was pursuing training that would equip him for ordination into ministry in the Presbyterian Church (USA), something that did occur in 1981. For those of us on the campus at that time, the presence of Jeb Stuart Magruder generated as much conversation as any topic raised and discussed in our classes and intensive workshops.

There were only two ways in which to respond to Magruder's presence at Princeton. One position, held by many at that time, was that his past life as a part of the Watergate scandal, his conviction on the charge of conspiracy to cover up a crime, and his subsequent federal prison sentence should have disqualified him from being a suitable candidate for the ordained ministry. Thus, he should have never been allowed admission into the seminary.

The second way that people thought about Magruder was a position that points directly to Moses and to the question being raised in this chapter. Doesn't God reserve the right to call into ministry any persons whom God may chose, whether or not there are other individuals in the church or in a seminary classroom who might reject or overlook or even hold such persons in contempt because of the immoral or illegal actions of their past?

Magruder offered his own answer to this question. He said to those who questioned whether his calling and ministry were authentic, "It is a characteristic of American life that there is redemption."[3] The miracle of the ministry is that God knows there is a shadow of the Moses/Magruder story in all of us. Any preacher who claims to be worthy or deserving of the task of being a preacher of the gospel of Jesus Christ based upon his or her own spotless and impeccable character is entirely unfit for the job! Those who are surprised that God has called them to this preaching ministry, despite everything we and God know about them, their past lives, and their own struggles with sin—those are the ones whom God can use.

Like Jeb Stuart Magruder, all preachers are to some degree the beneficiaries of God's redemptive love and God's gift of second chances at life.

Ananias of Damascus and Saul of Tarsus

There may be no better example of the conflict between the persons the church may choose to reject and the persons whom God may choose to call than the story in Acts 9, in which Ananias is told in a vision from Jesus: "Go to the house of Judas on Straight Street and ask for a man from Tarsus named Saul" (Acts 9:11, NIV). Ananias was being sent to lay hands on Saul and welcome him into the fellowship of the church. Notice that the initial response of Ananias was to remind Jesus about the past actions of Saul: "Lord, I have heard many reports about this man and all the harm he has done to your holy people in Jerusalem. And he has come here with authority from the chief priests to arrest all who call on your name" (Acts 9:13-14, NIV). In other words, Ananias was informing Jesus that Saul was not the right person, because Saul had a terrible reputation for attacking the very church that Jesus was trying to establish.

The response of Jesus to the concerns of Ananias points to the central claim of this chapter, namely, that God is free to choose people whom the church would overlook or reject. The Lord tells Ananias, "Go! This man is my chosen instrument to proclaim my name to the Gentiles and their kings and to the people of Israel" (v. 15, NIV). The reluctance to embrace Saul was not limited to Ananias. When Saul (not yet known as Paul) first began preaching about Jesus being the Messiah, verses 21-22 (NIV) say, "All those who heard him were astonished and asked, 'Isn't he the man who raised havoc in Jerusalem among those who call on this name? And hasn't he come here to take them as prisoners to the chief priests?' Yet Saul grew more and more powerful and baffled the Jews living in Damascus by proving that Jesus is Messiah."

The reluctance about Saul extended back to Jerusalem, because verse 26 (NIV) points out that "when he came to Jerusalem, he tried to join the disciples, but they were all afraid of him, not believing that he really was a disciple." It was not until Barnabas stepped forward and vouched both for Saul's conversion and for the power of his preaching in the name of Jesus that Saul was finally accepted by the apostles and the followers of Jesus in that city. What this story clearly reveals is that no preacher comes to this work of accepting the call to declare the gospel free of some past fault or flaw that others might use to argue against that preacher being used in God's service.

Sin Is Not a Problem Only for the Pew

Romans 3:23 should be at the heart of a preacher's understanding of the work we as preachers have been called to do: "All have sinned and fall short of the glory of God." I do not highlight this verse so that it can serve as the basis for what we should be preaching to others about their sinful lives. Rather, I lift it up to remind preachers that we ourselves are included in that verse. We who preach are numbered among "all have sinned."

I mentioned in the introduction of this book the conversation that a friend of mine had when word came out that he had been called to be a preacher. Someone who had known my friend since their childhood and through their years of young adulthood said to him, "You are not fit to be a preacher." My friend responded by saying, "I told God that same thing, but God decided to call me anyway."

Black suits and pulpit vestments can leave a congregation with an impression of a preacher based upon external observation. It does not matter how many robes, cassocks, academic hoods, or liturgical stoles preachers wear. None of those things resolve the issue at stake in this chapter and in this book, namely, that all of us who preach should claim for ourselves the sentiment of the classic hymn that says, "He snatched my feet from the miry clay . . . and placed them on a rock to stay."

Preachers should never judge fitness for ministry by what we see in the mirror on any given day, or by what glowing things are said about us as someone is introducing us to preach for some special occasion. We must remember that (in most cases) God had to bring us from certain places, deliver us from certain practices, and separate us from certain people, all of which may have loomed large in our past. It is not the purpose or the prerogative of this book to speculate as to what those past people, places, and practices might have been. The sole purpose of this book is to remind preachers about Romans 3:23 and about the fact that "all have sinned," and that includes us as preachers.

When Martin Luther King Jr. came to Chicago in 1966, he had a single objective in mind. While the immediate focus of that campaign was to challenge racial segregation in housing patterns in that city, the bigger issue was to use Chicago as proof of the fact that racism and segregation were not problems limited to the states of the former Confederacy. Racism and segregation were American problems that were as prevalent in the Midwest and the Northeast as they were in the Deep South. In fact, King was once heard stating during a television interview that the most hatred toward black people he had ever seen or felt was in Chicago and not Birmingham or Selma or Montgomery.

The same principle applies when it comes to the universal nature of sin and spiritual shortcomings. "All have sinned." The public revelations about nationally known preachers who have been accused or found guilty of sexual misconduct and financial fraud over the last several decades should be a reminder that all have sinned. Consider the example of the long-hidden but subsequently explosive exposure of child sexual abuse by dozens of Roman Catholic priests over the course of decades.

In fact, that example raises the question of what is worse: the sins of the preacher or the cover-up by the church? Paul Shanley, one of those defrocked Roman Catholic priests, was recently released after spending twelve years in prison for repeatedly raping a young boy during the 1980s.[4] Stories such as Shanley's resulted in the 2015 Oscar-winning motion picture entitled *Spotlight*, which looked at not only sexual abuse by the priests but also the systemic way in which the Roman Catholic diocese in Boston (and in other cities as well) covered up for these sexual predators. Many predator-priests were moved from one parish to another where their criminal sexual practices were often repeated.

In light of this scandal and far too many other news stories, there is no way to argue that sin is a problem for the people in the pew but not also a problem for the people in the pulpit. Yet, the fact remains that God reserves the right to call into or to restore into ministry anyone whom God chooses. It may well be that people in the church might not have chosen that person due to the sinfulness of their past. However, when it comes to the making of a preacher, it is sometimes the one who has strayed furthest away from God whom can be redeemed and forgiven and bring great glory to God.[5]

The question for this chapter is whether our sins should permanently exclude us from being used in God's service. Can people be redeemed through acts of repentance and restoration much as was the case with the chief tax collector named Zacchaeus in Luke 19:8? Here was a man who acknowledged the wrongs he committed, and then restored fourfold the money he had wrongfully gained. There are instances when restorative justice might be required as a first step toward being used in God's service, or as the basis for being readmitted after one has committed some grave offense.

In one notable instance, redemption and a return to full ministerial status was possible if ego and pride had not gotten in the way. In 1988 the internationally renowned televangelist Jimmy Swaggart was discovered to have engaged in behaviors that were inconsistent with his standing as a minister in the Assemblies of God denomination. In response to the public disclosure of what he had done, Swaggart went on his television program and tearfully confessed, "I have sinned against you, O Lord."[6] Leaders of the executive committee of the Assemblies of God imposed upon Swaggart a one-year suspension of his standing as a preacher in that denomination, as well as a two-year rehabilitation program to address his sexual misconduct. Upon completing that suspension, he would be restored to full ministerial standing. Despite what he had done, the national church leaders of the Assemblies of

God and his own local congregation were willing to restore Jimmy Swaggart to his ministry. This was a powerful example of a person being told that God could still use him despite the public nature of his sinful past.

However, rather than comply with the ruling of his denomination, largely because he needed the revenue generated by his television ministry to maintain his church and his broadcasting schedule, Swaggart defied his national church body and announced that he would return to the pulpit after only three months away from the ministry. In response, the denomination defrocked him, stripping him of any further standing as an Assemblies of God preacher.[7] In this instance, the legitimate church discipline that had been imposed was rejected by someone who, if he had waited the twelve months, might well have come back with a stronger testimony and a broader appeal than before.

Preachers Should Pay Attention to Pronouns

Another verse comes quickly to mind that preachers may well have used in sermons directed to one congregation or another. First John 1:10 (NIV) says, "If we claim we have not sinned, we make him out to be a liar and his word is not in us." Here is a verse where one of the disciples of Jesus and one of the apostles sent to preach the gospel to the world links himself to the reality of sin. Notice the pronouns used by John: "If *we* claim *we* have not sinned, *we* make him out to be a liar, and his word is not in *us*" (emphasis added). This is not a stern warning that should be delivered from the saints in the pulpit to the sinners in the pew. This is a stern warning for the pulpit as well as the pew. All of us—ALL OF US—are sinners saved by grace.

Our preaching should reflect the fact that we do not simply understand the temptations and haunting memories of past behaviors that may afflict others in our congregations. Our preaching should make clear that at some points we who preach are and have been struggling with sin *ourselves*. We are with Paul when he says in Romans 7:15-19 (NIV):

> I do not understand what I do. For what I want to do I do
> not do, but what I hate to do is what I do. And if I do what I
> do not want to do, I agree that the law is good. As it is, it is
> no longer I myself who do it, but it is sin living in me. For
> I know that good itself does not dwell in me, that is, in my
> sinful nature. For I have the desire to do what is good, but I
> cannot carry it out. For I do not do the good I want to do, but
> the evil I do not want to do—this I keep on doing.

Here Paul was laying bare his character conflict. He seemed unable to do what he knew was right, and he seemed unable to keep himself from doing what he knew was wrong. Whether driven by anger, personal prejudice, jealousy, greed, vengeance, lust, or misinformation, all people find themselves echoing the words of Paul. This was the confession of Jeb Magruder, who said, "Somewhere between my ambition and my ideals, I lost my ethical compass."[8] No preacher should consider oneself outside of this spiritual tug-of-war. We will be far better preachers if we avoid any notion of being beyond the reach of sin and Satan, and say these words instead: "It ain't my mother or my father, but it's me, O Lord, standing in the need of prayer."

Learn a Lesson from Peter and Judas

If the work of preaching were reserved only for people who have never broken a law, broken a promise, broken a heart, or broken open a whiskey bottle, there would be no one qualified by such a standard to preach the gospel. This is the fundamental difference between the contemporaneous experiences of Judas Iscariot and Simon Peter in the aftermath of the events in the Garden of Gethsemane on the night when Jesus was arrested and set on the path that would lead to Calvary and to crucifixion. They seem to have held two very different views of who was and was not qualified to be a servant of the Lord.

The name Judas has been consigned to infamy. No one names their child Judas. I am unaware of any church, city, hospital, school, airport, or religious order named in honor of Judas. I doubt that any real pet lover would give the name Judas to their cat or dog. Why is this the case? The easy answer would seem to be that Judas disqualified himself from all future honor and recognition because he betrayed Jesus in the Garden of Gethsemane. Through an agreement he entered that garnered him thirty pieces of silver in return, Judas kissed Jesus on the cheek on that fateful night, identifying his teacher and friend to those who had come that night to arrest him. Whatever the motives of Judas might have been, he quickly realized the error of his ways. He attempted to return the blood money he had received, and then he committed suicide because he believed he had done something he could not live with. Worse, he believed he had done something that could not possibly be forgiven, not by God, not by the other disciples, and not by himself.

Contrast the story of Judas Iscariot with the story of Simon Peter. Both were in the Garden of Gethsemane on the night when Jesus was arrested. Both "lost their ethical compass" that night. Judas lost his way when he betrayed Jesus, and Peter lost his way when he denied even knowing Jesus. It should be noted that what Judas did he did only once, while what Peter did was repeated three times, with each denial becoming increasingly emphatic. One could ask two questions based upon the behavior that night of Judas Iscariot and Simon Peter. The first question is whose behavior was more unfaithful: what Judas did once or what Peter did three times?

The second question is why the name of Peter has not suffered the same fate as the name of Judas. After all, unlike Judas, there are cities, colleges, airports, churches, and religious orders that proudly bear the name of Peter. Parents all over the world have given the name Peter to their children. Indeed, the pope of the Roman Catholic Church is said to stand in direct succession from Peter as bishop of the church in Rome. What is the difference between the legacy of Peter and the legacy of Judas?

The answer may be exactly what has been argued so far in this chapter: that God's redemptive love allows sinners to remain eligible for the service of the Lord no matter what their sin might have been. The difference between Judas and Peter is found in the fact that Peter lived long enough to discover the truth of that redemptive love. He lived long enough to learn that while he may have denied Jesus, Jesus was in no way prepared to deny him. According to Mark 16:7, while the body of Judas may have still been hanging from a tree, the body of Jesus had already been resurrected. The women who had come to the tomb to anoint the body of Jesus in accordance with Jewish burial practices discovered that his body was already gone. A person dressed in white then gave those women this instruction: "Go, tell his disciples and Peter, 'He is going ahead of you into Galilee. There you will see him, just as he told you'" (NIV).

What is interesting about this text is not what the women were told to do, but who those women were and to whom they were being sent. The women in question were Mary Magdalene, Mary the mother of Jesus, and Salome, who were also listed as being present at the crucifixion (Mark 15:40). These women knew Jesus, and they knew all his disciples. If the messenger dressed in white had said, "Go and tell his disciples," it is absolutely certain they would have told Peter as well. They did not need the specific reminder to include Peter in this announcement of the resurrection. These women knew all the disciples, and they would have told all of them, Peter included.

So why is there this specific reference to one disciple by name? Why does the messenger say, "and Peter"? This seems to have been the moment when Peter's past behavior was declared not to be an obstacle to his future service. "And Peter" was the signal to Peter as well as to the other disciples that Peter's weakness and faithlessness in denying Jesus were being set aside so that Peter's future ministry could get underway. God reserves the right to call into ministry anyone God chooses, including persons whose sinful past might have disqualified them in the eyes of everyone but God.

Is it possible that had Judas not committed suicide, if he had allowed time for God's grace to be directed to him as well as to Peter, then the name of Judas could also have been re-deemed? Is it possible that he could have been kept from the list of traitors rivaled only by the name of Benedict Arnold, who betrayed George Washington and the Continental Army during the Revolutionary War? It seems likely that if Peter could be forgiven and redeemed for what he did three times, what Judas did only once could also have been forgiven. Indeed, it begs the question that if God would not forgive Judas for what he did, then why do any of us believe that we would be treated differently and be forgiven of our sins?

Should Preachers Reveal the Sins of Their Past in Sermons?

One of the unresolved questions about preaching is if, and in what ways, we preachers should refer to ourselves in our sermons. How much time should we spend celebrating our accomplishments and reporting on every success we have ever known? How deeply should we delve into our sinful past in the context of a sermon? To what extent should we allow people to know who we were and how we might have behaved in ways that they might perceive as shocking and unbecoming of someone who is now a preacher? It is possible that, if we reveal too much about our past blunders and blemishes, then the people to whom we are preaching could begin to second-guess whether we are the kind of person and the kind of Christian they thought we are. In contemporary terms, there is such a thing as TMI, or *too much information*. How should that factor into our preaching?

I remember teaching a preaching class at the Ashland Seminary extension in Detroit, Michigan, sometime in the 1990s. Part of that course involved students delivering a sermon so that they could get some experience in preaching and receive some constructive feedback from the professor and from their peers. I will never forget one student who told us during his sermon about his twenty-year battle with heroin addiction. He told us about the five or six times he had overdosed and had to be taken to the emergency room because his life was in danger. Part of the feedback from the class was whether too much detail about his heroin habit had been revealed. Was this a case of TMI? Would it have been enough to offer some less specific description of his battle with addiction? Would a congregation that heard such a sermon respond positively to his message or negatively to his testimony?

There is a downside to sharing this kind of information in a sermon. It might plant seeds of doubt as to whether the preacher has overcome the addiction in question. The sensational nature of such a testimony might distract from the biblical message that the preacher is attempting to communicate. While this is an extreme case of some of the past and present behaviors that might be part of a preacher's journey, it is because such revelations can have an unpredictable effect on listeners that many preachers avoid referring to themselves in any way in their sermons.

On the other hand, there is an upside to such transparency. It is possible that the sermon could be extremely helpful for those who were battling with addiction themselves, and who could be encouraged by the fact that the preacher understood their predicament and had finally beaten addiction. Someone in the congregation could have said, "If the preacher can beat addiction, then so can I." It is true that "all have sinned and fallen short of the glory of God." The question here is how much of ourselves and our own life's journey should be revealed in our sermons?

A Character Test for Preachers: Are We Models or Mirrors?

In considering how much of ourselves should be revealed in our sermons, I offer a principle I learned from James A. Sanders, who was my Old Testament professor in seminary. He employed the concept of "models" and "mirrors." In the context of the Bible, he asked which biblical characters could legitimately offer themselves as models of the kind of life that others should live. Which characters had lived in such a way that, no matter where we found them in the biblical story, they had never said or done anything that could lead to trouble for those who attempted to model their behavior?

As great as Abraham was, he did lie to Pharaoh, telling him that Sarah, his wife, was really his sister, exposing Sarah to a potentially adulterous encounter. As great a king as David was, he did commit adultery with Bathsheba and send Uriah the Hittite off to his death as a way of trying to cover up the pregnancy that ensued from what he thought would be a one-night stand. As central as Rebekah was to the biblical story, she did seek to deceive her husband, Isaac, and to actively work to deny her son Esau of his birthright so that it could fall to her favorite son, Jacob, thus creating animosity between her two sons that would last for decades. The list of biblical characters continued, and no one except Jesus himself could be held up as a model for our behavior. Even Paul said, "Follow my example, as I follow the example of Christ" (1 Corinthians 11:1, NIV).

The same principle holds true for the character of preachers; none of us is qualified to be a model for how others should live their lives. We are too prone to get caught up in the sins of the flesh set forth in Galatians 5:19-21, which include jealousy, selfishness, fits of rage, sexual immorality, hatred, discord, and envy. We are often tempted by the behaviors set forth in Romans 1, which is often employed by those who are quick to condemn same-sex relationships—but how convenient it is to ignore what else is found in that chapter, including murder, strife, deceit, malice, gossip, arrogance, boastfulness, disobedience of parents, and an absence of mercy and love.

Dr. Sanders was correct: only Jesus can serve as the consistent and unfailing model for the behavior of others. I am afraid to associate myself with Paul's invitation to "follow my example, as I follow the example of Jesus." I want to urge people to follow the example of Jesus and leave myself out of the modeling role altogether.

While Sanders could easily demonstrate that only Jesus qualified to be a model in terms of demonstrating behaviors that others could and should follow, he asserted that every human being can serve as a mirror. A mirror involves those biblical characters in whom we can see our own faults and failures reflected. If models say this person's example reflects how we should live, a mirror is a person whose life reflects the struggles and shortfalls that we are actually living. When we think of ourselves as mirrors, we can see ourselves and our sinful behaviors reflected in the behavior of Abraham, David, and Rebekah, Judas and Peter, Moses and others.

Therefore, preachers should never refer to themselves in their sermons as models for their hearers and congregations to emulate, because upon closer scrutiny we are thrown back on Romans 3:23, "All have sinned." However, every preacher knows there have been times when our lives perfectly mirrored the same struggles we see going on in the lives of those to whom we preach. It could be helpful to our listeners if we as preachers chose to share some of our struggles with temptation, or anger, or fear, or greed, or personal prejudice.

I have a sermon entitled, "What Price Would You Pay to Be Popular?" The sermon is based on the behavior of Pontius Pilate when he presided over the trial of Jesus (Mark 15:6-15). It is clear in that passage that Pilate did not think Jesus had done anything deserving of death. Pilate could have ordered Jesus to be released, because he knew those clamoring for the death of Jesus did so out of jealousy (Mark 15:10). He could have stood by his conviction that Jesus had done nothing wrong (Mark 15:14). Instead, he handed Jesus over to be flogged and then crucified. And he did that for one simple, selfish, sinful reason; "Pilate, wishing to satisfy the crowd, released Barabbas for them; and after flogging Jesus, he handed him over to be crucified" (Mark 15:15). Jesus Christ, the Lamb of God who takes away the sins of the world, was sent off to face the cruelest form of death yet conceived by the human mind, because Pontius Pilate was more interested in satisfying the crowd than he was in following his own conscience. That was the price he was willing to pay to be popular with the people.

The point of that sermon was not to point a finger at Pilate as if he were somehow unique in his willingness to place popularity over personal conviction. The role of the preacher with this text is not to hover over Pilate as if Pilate and we who talk about him do not have much in common. In this sermon, I recount the many times in my own life when I did the exact same thing in principle, if not in detail. I have placed my desire to satisfy a crowd ahead of my knowledge that what I was doing was wrong and un-Christian. I did not need to be told that I was sinning. I was clear about that. However, there was some crowd whose approval I wanted so badly that I was prepared to violate my own conscience to gain the favor of that crowd.

I could not stand before a congregation or before God and pretend to be a model whose conduct others should follow. But I could stand there as a person whose life mirrors the same faults and flaws that are found in the biblical characters that we sometimes demonize too quickly. At stake is not whether characters such as Pontius Pilate paid too high a price to gain popularity. At stake is the confession that I have done the exact same thing repeatedly, paying too high a price to win approval from someone other than God. Returning to the central point of this chapter and this book, God calls us into ministry despite all the faults and failures in our lives that are mirrored in the lives of biblical characters like Moses. Understanding this fact is essential in the making of a preacher.

■ ■ ■

Notes

1. Jeb Stuart Magruder, *From Power to Peace* (Dallas: Word, 1978).
2. Godfrey Hodgson, "Jeb Magruder Obituary," *The Guardian*, May 24, 2014, 1.
3. Ibid., 4.
4. Katharine Q. Seelye, "Defrocked Priest Is About to Be Freed Amid Renewed Fury," *The New York Times*, July 26, 2017, 1, https://www.nytimes.com/2017/07/26/us/boston-priest-paul-shanley-sex-abuse.html.
5. When the scandal is related to criminal offenses, especially concerning the abuse of children by church leaders, there is an ethical need for congregations and denominational bodies to remove these leaders from further pastoral work, and there is a legal imperative to isolate them from any future contact with children. That is something that churches and judicatories need to consider on a case-by-case basis, in consultation with law enforcement or other legal counsel.
6. Wayne King, "Jimmy Swaggart Says He Has Sinned; Will Step Down," *The New York Times*, February 22, 1988, 1, https://www.nytimes.com/1988/02/22/us/swaggart-says-he-has-sinned-will-step-down.html.

7. The Associated Press, "Church Defrocks Swaggart for Rejecting Its Punishment," *The New York Times*, April 8, 1988, 1, https://www.nytimes.com/1988/04/09/us/church-defrocks-swaggart-for-rejecting-its-punishment.html.
8. Hodgson, 4.

Chapter 4

More Questions of Character

But Moses said to the LORD, "O my Lord, I have never been eloquent, neither in the past nor even now that you have spoken to your servant; but I am slow of speech and slow of tongue." Then the LORD said to him, "Who gives speech to mortals? Who makes them mute or deaf, seeing or blind? Is it not I, the LORD? Now go, and I will be with your mouth and teach you what you are to speak." —Exodus 4:10-12

■ ■ ■

In the previous chapter, we focused exclusively on the question of Moses' character as it was defined by the sins of his past. However, there are two other important characteristics involved in the call of Moses that are instructive as we consider the making of a preacher. We will explore those traits together in this chapter. The first was Moses' self-awareness that he was not an eloquent speaker and was "slow of speech and slow of tongue" (Exodus 4:10). The second is the fact that Moses was eighty years old when God called him. Thus, we have two questions to be considered in the making of a preacher: (1) Is there any physical disability or skill limitation that might result in an automatic exemption from being used by God? (2) Is there an age beyond which a person is no longer useful to or eligible for divine service?

There are many professions from which persons can be excluded based upon factors of age, health, or physical ability. This would include certain positions or branches of the military, the roster of a professional sports team, or opportunities in the entertainment industry. In each of those areas, age or size or strength and stamina might rule them out. A person seeking a tenure track position in an academic institution may not reach that rank if he or she started the teaching career too late in life. Bad vision can prevent someone from obtaining a license to pilot an aircraft or to drive a commercial vehicle.

However, there are also some churches that would never consider hiring as its senior pastor someone who exceeded a certain age. There was a very prominent church in New York City that invited me to apply for the position of senior pastor. However, when they realized that I was much older than they had assumed, and that I had far fewer years of ministry service ahead of me than I had behind me, they quickly moved on to consider a much younger candidate. As they soon discovered, what they had gained in terms of youth they had lost in terms of experience.

The same can be said about a church calling someone as senior pastor who was challenged when it came to verbal communication. When I was called to interview for the position of pastor of Antioch Baptist Church in Cleveland, Ohio in 1986, I was not aware of a debate that had been going on within the search committee. The job description that was initially drafted said, "Preaching skills preferred but not required." That line met with immediate resistance from many members who thought that in the process of calling a pastor they were also intent upon calling a preacher! One member of the committee was reported to have asked others on the committee, "Are you all suggesting that if the candidate cannot preach effectively that we would seriously consider that person to be our pastor?"

Here again, the story of the call of Moses is a reminder that God has and will call persons into ministry whom people in the church would pass over.

The Testimony of One Who Stuttered

I am especially intrigued by the excuse offered by Moses that he was slow of tongue and slow of speech. I had a great struggle with a similar problem prior to and long after I sensed my call to the ministry. Through most of my elementary school years I had a pronounced stutter and lisp. I had a very difficult time speaking in public, because my words either rushed out too fast for others to hear, or too slowly for others to follow, or too incoherently because I slurred on the "S" sound. (I sounded just like the cartoon character Daffy Duck!) The slurring problem was corrected by a speech therapist who worked with me at Paul Cornell Elementary School in Chicago. It was a matter of the placement of the tongue behind and not between the top and bottom row of teeth. I have never lisped again past the age of thirteen.

However, the stuttering and the rapid speech lasted well into my thirties. I empathized with the character of King George VI of England in the movie *The King's Speech* as he struggled to get his words out. I knew what I wanted to say, but I could not get my mind and my mouth coordinated. Words either would not come out at all, or they would come pouring out far too quickly for me to be understood. Strangely enough, this was never a problem in a social setting among friends and neighbors. But when called upon to read or speak in public, I was a bundle of nerves.

I was invited to read the Scripture for my baccalaureate service at Union Theological Seminary of New York City in 1973. The distinguished theologian Paul Lehmann was the preacher for that occasion. He selected Exodus 32:1-6 as his text, the story of Aaron and the golden calf, and he asked me to read that text during the service. I should have said no and told him why. However, as I said, I did not have this problem while speaking or asking a question in class, so he had no idea I was struggling with this problem.

As soon as the text was assigned I began the practice of reading it aloud to myself. Then I read it aloud to several of my classmates as we sat in a student lounge. No problem as I read in a small room full of supportive and encouraging classmates. What happened on the day of the service was another matter altogether. I got to the phrase that read, "As for this Moses, the man who brought us up out of the land of Egypt, we do not know what has become of him." Those words poured out like a torrent, with one word following so closely upon the next that it is doubtful that anyone present understood what I was saying.

It has been almost forty-five years since that day, and I can still recall the fear and anxiety that gripped me as I struggled to enunciate clearly that passage in front of my fellow graduates, our assembled families and friends who had gathered for the two-day graduation exercises, and before the entire faculty of the seminary. The joy of my graduation was overshadowed by the embarrassment I felt as I struggled to read that passage in public. What made that experience more poignant was that on the next day, during the commencement service held inside Riverside Church at which Gardner Taylor was the speaker, I was awarded the Richard Hudnut Award as the best preacher in the class of 1973. It seemed that I could speak the words that I had written for my sermons, but I was not yet able to read in public words found in Scripture or a litany or a responsive reading.

As recently as my pastoral years in Cleveland, Ohio, between 1986 and 2011, this problem with reading printed texts in a public setting filled me with anxiety. On any given Sunday, I would labor to read the Scripture text for that week without stumbling over my words. At funeral services when it was time to read the obituary aloud, or to read Scripture and bits of poetry during the service and at the graveside, it was a long time before I felt comfortable doing so. Because of my visibility as the pastor of a prominent congregation in that city, persons seeking election to a political office would invite me to give them my endorsement. If a news reporter interviewed me to ask why I was endorsing a certain person, and if I could answer in my own words, there was no real problem. When the candidate would urge me to make my endorsement in the form of reading from a printed text provided by their campaign committee, it was another matter entirely. It would require one taping after another and after another before I could manage to read those words slowly enough to be understood by the radio or television engineers.

The point is that God knew that I stuttered when I was called into the ministry. It took almost twenty years after my call for me to feel comfortable reading any printed text other than my own sermon manuscripts in public. In full disclosure, the primary reason why I worked so hard to learn how to preach without a manuscript is because trying to read from a manuscript that I had written would generate the problems with my speech patterns that I was working so hard to overcome.

It may not be apparent to people who have observed me speaking in public over the last thirty years that I was ever slow of tongue and slow of speech. The truth is that I was someone whom God should have overlooked and passed by for a profession that involved regular doses of public speaking. What happened was that from my speech therapy classes in elementary school, to my decades-long struggles with reading printed texts in public settings, I was involved in a case study on the making of a preacher.

Learning from Clay Evans

As serious as my speech impediment might have been, it was nothing compared to the experience of Clay Evans, who was the pastor of Fellowship Baptist Church in my hometown of Chicago during the time when I experienced my call to ministry. Clay Evans was known both for his preaching and his singing style which was described as "blues preaching" which Zach Mills defines as: "An orality—a vast matrix of speaking tones, singing techniques, styles of communication, vernacular expressions, and rhetorical devices—shaped the ways black southern migrants in Chicago expressed themselves in secular and religious spaces."[1]

Blues preaching was a spirituals-and-blues inspired tradition of preaching that circulated throughout various parts of the South in the late nineteenth and twentieth centuries. Blues preachers became significant pillars in African American communities in northern cities like Chicago and Detroit. The skills of the blues preacher were not acquired in a classroom . . . they were forged in the fiery furnace of racism, brutality, and suffering African Americans experienced in the South in the early 1900s.[2]

Second only to Clarence LaVaughn (C. L.) Franklin of Detroit who was known as the "man with the million-dollar voice" because of the popularity of the recordings of his sermons and singing,[3] Clay Evans was the most popular preacher in the country due to his weekly radio and TV broadcasts, and his recordings with Chess Records.[4]

What warrants this reference to Clay Evans is the fact that he could not speak, he was mute for the first three years of his life.[5] Who would ever have imagined that one of the greatest preachers and gospel singers of all time would have started out mute, living on a sharecropping plantation in the segregated South? The answer points back to Moses, the fugitive from Egyptian justice who resisted his call to ministry on the grounds that he was slow of tongue and speech (Exodus 4:10). God can call and equip anyone whom God chooses to use in divine service no matter their lack of eloquence or speaking ability.

Walkers, Wheelchairs, and Other Challenges

There are many more things than a speech impediment that could have served as a reason for God to pass over someone, or for someone to say to themselves that they should not acknowledge a call to ministry. As president of Colgate Rochester Crozer Divinity School, and as a professor of preaching at other schools over a period of thirty years, I have had the privilege of observing hundreds of students earn their Master of Divinity and Doctor of Ministry degrees. In the CRCDS class of 2017 there were students who came to receive their degrees pushing themselves in wheelchairs or leaning on walkers. The physical design of the school did not make their lives any easier. They could not reach any office without first maneuvering stairs and/or lifts. They could not enter the library or reading room, the chapel, the dining hall, or even the student lounge without being challenged by the same problem.

Yet, those students were the most faithful in chapel attendance. They made their way to the refectory for meals. You would often see their wheelchairs parked outside of a classroom as evidence that they were determined not to let a physical challenge become an obstacle to answering God's call to the ministry. There was not a dry eye in the Asbury First United Methodist Church of Rochester where our 2017 commencement service was held when one of those students who was physically challenged was given the award from the faculty for being the graduating student with the most promise for pastoral ministry. He is now serving as a deacon on the staff of an Episcopal church in Rochester, New York. Whether a person is slow of tongue or slow of step, God reserves the right to call anyone God chooses to serve in ministry wherever God chooses.

There is a pastor of a Roman Catholic congregation in Rochester, New York, who has both a speech impediment and a hearing impairment. When I attended a funeral at that church for a member of the seminary community, it was apparent that this priest was a pastor of the highest order. His eulogy was both comforting and humorous. When he presided over the Mass he was fully connected with the grieving family and the assembled congregation. At the end of the service he approached me to say that he had taken a long break from his doctoral studies at CRCDS, and he hoped to return very soon.

He did return for the intensive courses in the summer of 2017. There were two persons who took turns providing sign language services in his classes, in the chapel, in the dining hall, and places in between. Like the students in the master of divinity program, this doctoral student sought no exceptions due to his hearing and speech challenges in terms of classroom attendance or the deadline for turning in assignments. He sees himself as being called to ministry just like everybody else in the student body who is numbered among the "temporarily able." I will have a student in one of my upcoming doctoral seminars who will also need the use of a sign language interpreter throughout the day. They do this because they are convinced that God has called them to the ministry and that God knew about their physical challenges before calling them by name.

How Old Is Too Old?

Exodus 7:7 states, "Moses was eighty years old and Aaron was eighty-three when they spoke to Pharaoh." What does it say both about God and about Moses that God called an eighty-year-old man into service, and that eighty-year-old man never once used his advanced age as an excuse not to embrace what God was calling on him to do? Moses said he was slow of tongue and slow of speech, but he never said that he was too old. Moses wondered whether the people would believe him when he told them what God had said to him, but he never wondered aloud if he was too old to take on that assignment. Moses was obviously concerned that Pharaoh might not, probably would not believe him and agree to release the Hebrews from slavery in Egypt. Remarkably, the one thing Moses never said, suggested, or acknowledged in any way was that being eighty years old was too old to respond to God's call to duty.

In fact, there are two interwoven issues at stake when it comes to the call of Moses at the age of eighty. The first was God's willingness to call him at that advanced age, and the second was Moses' vigor to eventually accept his calling. Moses might not have desired to go back to Egypt, but despite his age he still had something to offer that could be useful in the service of God.

In practical terms, it would have made more sense for God to have called Moses when he was forty years old and still living in Egypt. True enough, he had killed an Egyptian overseer who had been brutalizing Hebrew slaves. However, God could surely have protected Moses from any retribution through a display of some of the power that God would later display through the plagues that finally broke the resistance of Pharaoh. At the age of forty, Moses would have had more energy to apply to his assignment. He would have had more status among the Egyptians as one known to them who had been raised in the royal palace. He would surely have enjoyed immense popularity among the Hebrews as a former prince of Egypt who was now working for their liberation. Hebrews

11:24-25 (NIV) almost suggests this possibility when it says, "By faith Moses, when he had grown up, refused to be known as the son of Pharaoh's daughter. He chose to be mistreated along with the people of God rather than to enjoy the fleeting pleasures of sin."

Hebrews 11 does go on to observe that Moses would eventually flee from and then return to Egypt. None of that is being disputed. The only thing being observed here is that Moses was available to be used in the service of God four decades before he was finally called into service. For whatever reason, God waited until Moses, a slow-of-speech fugitive from justice, was eighty years old before calling him.

Older Students Are Flooding Seminary Classrooms

Moses' story begs the question, is there any age beyond which persons should no longer be considered for a ministry assignment or a call to preach? The answer to that question can be found in seminary classrooms and minister-in-training programs across the country. A 2013 article in *The Wall Street Journal* entitled "For Second Careers, A Leap of Faith," pointed to the growing number of persons in their fifties and sixties who are "putting aside thoughts of retirement and heading to theological school, where they've become the fastest-growing age group in recent years."[6] During my own teaching career spanning more than thirty-five years at New Brunswick Theological Seminary, New York Theological Seminary, Princeton Theological Seminary, Ashland Theological Seminary, and now Colgate Rochester Crozer Divinity School, I have seen this pattern develop.

I have seen retired physicians, dentists, public school teachers, engineers, architects, contractors, career military service members, active and retired professional athletes, former police officers, and persons who worked in many other professions and vocations who sensed a call to ministry later in life and enrolled in seminary to earn graduate degrees in theological studies, religion, or divinity. In fact, in the summer 2017 I preached the sermon for an eighty-year-old alumnus of CRCDS whose ordination in one denomination was being publicly recognized by another group, primarily because that second denomination had a more open policy when it came to accepting women in ministry. As every seminary president and dean can attest, there is a steady decline in the number of young people coming straight out of college and into seminary like I did in 1970. But there *is* a steady increase in the number of older persons enrolling in all our seminaries and divinity schools.

Pope Saint John XXIII National Seminary near Boston, Massachusetts, is a Roman Catholic seminary that specializes in training second-career persons to become priests. The school has "a mission to prepare mature candidates for the priesthood. The average student age is 48 . . . they admit students between the ages of 30 and 60."[7] The school's vocation liaison states:

> **They sacrifice a lot to come here. In many cases they are very accomplished and have had the kind of lifestyle that accompanies that status. They give it all up to move to a campus and spend four years living in a room that is 8 by 12 and has shared bathroom facilities. The chances of going back to their more comfortable lives are slim. Unlike traditional students who are young enough to pursue other careers if they decide ministry isn't for them, mature candidates have made such a striking shift late in life that going back is not a real option. They're taking a huge risk, and they take it in faith.[8]**

Today, many of our students are employed full-time and attending seminary part-time, or they have retired or resigned from one career path in order to start down a new path they believe will bring more meaning to their lives. *The Wall Street Journal* article offered a possible answer for why persons might answer a call to ministry later in their lives. It quotes the philosopher William James, who said, "If the greatest use of a life is to spend it for something that will outlast it," few paths seem to offer more rewards than joining the clergy and related fields.[9]

It must be noted that many persons enter the ministry later in life, not because the call just came to them later in life but because they had been running from or denying that call for many years until something caused them to finally say yes to God. That is one of the findings of the collection of call stories edited by William Myers, *God's Yes Was Louder Than My No*.[10]

The story about the Roman Catholic seminary mentioned above offers confirmation about God calling people who take a long time to respond.

> **Seminary President Brian Kiely stated that "the call to ministry can exist for decades before a man responds affirmatively to it." . . . Case in point, John Maksym, the Navy's long-serving Judge Adjutant General and member of the seminary's class of 2018 says, "The Holy Spirit pursued me. As years went by, I realized it was time. I finally had to say yes, because sooner or later He's going to get His way."[11]**

There is an ongoing discussion within families and among churches about the age for retirement of members of the clergy. That conversation is over the question of the age at which a person should decide to leave the work of ministry behind. How interesting it is to note that another conversation is underway at the same time, namely, what is the age beyond which one is too old to enter some form of ministry? If one is informed by the call story of Moses, then the answer may well be that there is no age beyond which God cannot and will not call someone into ministry, however narrow or specialized that form of ministry might prove to be. Being a senior pastor or a full-time member of a church staff is not the only form that ministry can take. If reaching a certain advanced age becomes a deterrent to a older person being engaged in ministry, there are a host of other areas where age need not be a factor. Working with a prison ministry, teaching a weekly Bible class, being a supply preacher in one's own church or at some other church are all possibilities.

One Final Characteristic of Moses

Outside of Moses' call story in Exodus 2, two other biblical sources offer us a glimpse into his call and character. One source is Hebrews 11:24-28, which has already been referenced in this chapter. The other source comes from Acts 7:17-34, as part of the sermon delivered by Stephen before he was stoned to death. Among the things that Stephen noted about Moses and his character is the fact that "Moses was instructed in all the wisdom of the Egyptians" (7:22). Far from being a humble shepherd from the back side of Mount Horeb, Moses was a person with a solid intellectual foundation.

R. Alan Cole writes, "With the possible exceptions of Solomon, Daniel and Nehemiah, no Old Testament character had such training. Study of law would probably have been one aspect of any such education. Hammurabi's code, for instance, was widely studied and annotated by Egyptian scribes, so that Moses may have been well acquainted with it."[12] Cole goes on to say that "all this was the other side of God's preparation."[13] It is very likely that Moses could embrace the concept of divine laws from God written on stone tablets because of his earlier familiarity with the Code of Hammurabi, a Babylonian legal code that dated back to the eighteenth-century BCE and the days of Abraham.

It is also likely that there are some parallels to be drawn between the call and character of Moses and that of Saul of Tarsus. Both brought something to the task that few if any others of their time and place also possessed; formal training within the highest ranks of their respective sociocultural contexts. Moses was a product of the Egyptian empire, and Saul was trained within the Greco-Roman world.

Formal Training Is an Appropriate Response to the Call

As a seminary president and professor, I am inclined to embrace this aspect of the character of Moses as a way to encourage everyone who answers God's call to serve to also embrace the notion of gaining as much training for this job as possible. For those who are able, I strongly invite them to pursue their preparation and training through enrollment in and graduation from an accredited theological school. At a time when the people in the pews are pursuing more and more education in order to advance within their careers, it is foolish to think that they do not expect the same rigorous training in their pastors and preachers.

I make this point in an essay, "Why Seminary Training Is Important," written for the American Baptist Churches in 2017. I make the case that in 2 Timothy 2:2 (NIV), Paul places a heavy emphasis on preparation for ministry. He speaks about "entrusting" the word to "reliable" people who will be "qualified" to teach others. In 2 Timothy 2:15 (NIV) he asserts that preachers of the faith should "study" so they can be "approved" as persons who "correctly handle" the word of truth.[14]

People's faith is sharpened and nurtured when they are equipped to see the connections between the issues that are being discussed in the world around them and the values being promoted within the church. People in the pews need to know how their faith speaks to the issues of human sexuality, global warming and the environment, the terrible power of nuclear weapons, living a faithful Christian life in an increasingly interfaith global community, and various medical issues ranging from euthanasia and how life should end to attempts to produce genetically designed babies. People certainly need to understand how to practice their faith at a time when the nation's political norms and standards are being uprooted and overturned by a president who may be the most ill-equipped person ever to hold that office. There has never been a time when having a trained and learned clergy has been more important. As my friend and mentor, William A. Jones Jr., said to me many years ago, "The pulpit needs people with as many degrees as can be earned."

Learning Is Not Limited to a Classroom

I also fully understand that not everyone who feels called to ministry is inclined toward or able to pursue formal training in a classroom setting. Not everyone who is called into the ministry can afford the costs of a formal seminary education. Not everyone who is called into the ministry, especially when they are called somewhat later in their lives, has the time and schedule flexibility to enroll in a weeks-long and years-long academic program. Going to the best seminary in the country is no guarantee that a person will later prove to have a productive ministry career. Similarly, not going to seminary is not a guarantee that a person will fail when it comes to being an effective pastor or preacher or church leader.

However, not "going to school" and not "sitting in a classroom on a regular basis" is not an acceptable excuse for failing to pursue some form of education by other means and methods. There are special courses of study that might result in a certificate of some sort. There are endless workshops at national conventions and at pastors' conferences that occur across the country and throughout the year. There are correspondence courses that provide guided readings and instruction. In the twenty-first century, it is possible to access quality information and instruction without stepping outside your front door.

Study to Show Yourself Approved

The biblical phrase "Study to show yourself approved" is not only an important challenge coming from Paul to Timothy in 2 Timothy 2:15 (KJV). It is also the title of a chapter in Adam Bond's book I've Been Called—Now What?[15] That book in its entirety is a wonderful addition to the literature dealing with the call to Christian ministry. The chapter being referenced here focuses on the issue of training and preparation for ministry after one has been called. Recognizing that not all persons can or will attend seminary, Bond sets forth four possible approaches for training for ministry.

The first is what he calls a ministry apprenticeship in which a younger preacher seeks out the guidance and direction of an established pastor. Using an analogy from Star Wars, Bond suggests that a younger minister "may connect with a master to learn the ways of the Force."[16] The second approach involves attendance at denominational conferences and events.

Bond notes that "these events offer ministers a space to learn, exchange ideas, and develop ministry gifts and tools."[17] For some younger preachers, attendance at such conferences now seems to take precedence over attendance at denominational conventions.

Bond's third approach is attendance at a Bible college where the curriculum may be more focused on careers in ministry, such as pastors, preachers, missionaries, or youth leaders. Since most Bible colleges offer only an undergraduate degree, they might be a stepping stone to Bond's fourth approach to training for ministry, which is pursuing a seminary degree through a two- or three-year graduate program.[18] Whichever of these four approaches a person may choose for study after they have been called, Bond offers these words of encouragement: "Such preparation will not only bless you; it will touch the people who await your ministry."[19]

Consider the Example of C. L. Franklin

By one means or another, persons who have been called to preach should seek to provide themselves with the best training available to them. African American preachers have idolized Clarence LaVaughn (C. L.) Franklin for decades. They both celebrate and seek to emulate his preaching style, popularly referred to as whooping. When you hear some of the soulful notes being generated by his even-more-famous daughter, Aretha Franklin, you get a sense of what whooping in the context of a sermon sounds like. Franklin was equally famous for his own singing voice and for the way he incorporated actual singing into his preaching. He was so successful as a preacher/singer that he signed a recording contract with Chess Records and became known as "the man with the million-dollar voice," because that was how much money his recordings generated through national sales in the 1960s.[20]

One wonders if many of those same preachers who so eagerly emulate the preaching style of C. L. Franklin are just as eager to emulate his thirst for and constant quest for education. Everywhere his pastoral ministry took him, he sought out a school nearby where he could further his education.

When he was serving a church in Memphis he attended Lemoyne College. When he moved to serve a church in Buffalo, New York, Franklin enrolled at the University of Buffalo. That thirst for continuing education is part of what would lift him from being a sharecropper in Mississippi to one of the most beloved preachers of the twentieth century. Let us all go and do likewise! Or as Howard Thurman's autobiography is entitled, we should serve God "with head and heart."[21]

In Memory of My Uncle James

I want to end by referring to the path to learning taken by my uncle James B. Alford, who was pastor of Progressive Church of God in Christ in Maywood, Illinois, for forty-four years. For most of those years, COGIC did not place much of an emphasis on formal training for their clergy. That denomination seemed to follow the example of their founder, Charles H. Mason, who dropped out of Arkansas Baptist College because he was uncomfortable with its focus on a critical approach to the study of Scripture. He also feared that formal training would "dampen the enthusiastic form of worship and preaching he had learned from and experienced among former slaves in the South. Preserving that authentic religious enthusiasm of his youth would be among Mason's primary concerns for the rest of his life."[22]

Despite the lack of emphasis given to formal education within COGIC, James Alford managed to amass one of the most impressive private libraries on biblical and theological studies I have ever seen outside of the office of a tenured seminary professor. His library was not for showing off to people who visited him in his church office. His library was on the second floor of his home where few people outside of his family would ever go. He spent endless hours in that library in his own attempt to be "instructed in all the wisdom of Egypt." I had this point confirmed for me when my mother and Uncle James, who was her older brother, went on a college campus tour with me in 1966.

My mother went to the financial aid office to see what kind of assistance they would be able to provide at a time when the cost of tuition was an astronomical amount of $33 per credit hour. Uncle James went straight to the college library. First, he roamed through the stacks in the religion and philosophy sections to see what the school had in its collection. When he did not see some of the things he thought should be there, he approached one of the librarians to inquire why a certain group of titles was not included. Not only were the librarians responsive to his informed inquiry, but many of the titles he suggested to them soon appeared on the shelves of my college library.

It should also be noted that soon after the death of C. H. Mason in 1961, the Church of God in Christ established a seminary that now bears his name. The C. H. Mason Theological Seminary is one of schools that constitute the Interdenominational Theological Center (ITC) in Atlanta, Georgia.[23] Even groups that may at first have been resistant to pursuing formal education as preparation for ministry now realize the benefits of "being instructed in all the wisdom of the Egyptians."

Whether a person receives formal theological training, is self-taught, or is set on a path of lifelong learning, there is one more classroom that all preachers need to visit. Acts 4:13 focuses on Peter and John, who had been arrested after preaching about Jesus in Jerusalem. Upon being released from prison, they were brought before the religious leaders of that city. The text says, "When they saw the courage of Peter and John and realized that they were unschooled, ordinary men, they were astonished and they took note that these men had been with Jesus" (NIV).

No amount of theological training or self-study can serve as a substitute for "being with Jesus." Unlike Peter and John, we have not had the opportunity to be with Jesus during his earthly pilgrimage, but we must find ways to be with Jesus in study and prayer and meditation. The old hymn says, "I come to the garden alone . . . and he walks with me and he talks with me, and he tells me I am his own. And the joy we share as we tarry there, none other has ever known." Preachers need to find frequent and regular ways and times to "be with Jesus." This, too, is part of what is involved in the making of a preacher.

▓ ▓ ▓

Notes

1. Zach Mills, *The Last of the Blues Preachers* (Minneapolis, MN: Fortress Press, 2018), 1.
2. Ibid., 5.
3. Marvin A. McMickle, "Franklin, Clarence LaVaughn (C. L.)," in *An Encyclopedia of African American Christian Heritage* (Valley Forge, PA: Judson Press, 2002), 58–59.
4. Zach Mills, *The Last of the Blues Preachers* (Minneapolis, MN: Fortress Press, 2018), 176.
5. Ibid., 5.
6. Anne Tergesen, "For Second Careers, a Leap of Faith," *The Wall Street Journal*, May 19, 2013, https://www.wsj.com/articles/SB1000142412 78873237410045784168829613644 50.
7. Jay Blossom and Holly G. Miller, "Seminary Specializes in Second-Career Students," *In Trust* (Summer 2017), 4.
8. Ibid.
9. Tergesen, "For Second Careers."
10. William H. Myers, *God's Yes Was Louder Than My No* (Grand Rapids, MI: Eerdmans, 1994), pp. 63–64.
11. Blossom and Miller, 5.
12. R. Alan Cole, *Exodus*, Tyndale Old Testament Commentaries (Downers Grove, IL: InterVarsity Press, 2008), 65–66.
13. Ibid., 65.
14. Marvin A. McMickle, "Why Seminary Training Is Important," *Tomorrow: Newsletter of the MMBB of American Baptist Churches*, https://www.mmbb.org/financial-planning/newsletters/tomorrow/ tomorrow-newsletter-4th-quarter-2017/.
15. Adam L. Bond, *I've Been Called: Now What?* (Valley Forge, PA: Judson Press, 2012), 53ff.
16. Ibid., 55.
17. Ibid.
18. Ibid.
19. Ibid., 68.
20. Marvin A. McMickle, *An Encyclopedia of African American Christian Heritage*, 59.
21. Howard Thurman, *With Head and Heart* (New York: Harcourt Brace & Company, 1979).
22. Marvin A. McMickle, "Mason, Charles Harrison (C. H.)," in *An Encyclopedia of African American Christian Heritage* (Valley Forge, PA: Judson Press, 2002), 33.
23. Marvin A. McMickle, "Interdenominational Theological Center (ITC)," in *An Encyclopedia of African American Christian Heritage* (Valley Forge, PA: Judson Press, 2002), 251.

Chapter 5

The Content of the Message

When Israel was in Egypt's land, let my people go.
Oppressed so hard they could not stand, let my people go.
Go down Moses, way down in Egypt land,
Tell old Pharaoh to let my people go.
—African American spiritual

■ ■ ■

As dramatic as the call story of Moses might have been, his place in history is not primarily connected to the events at the burning bush on Mount Horeb. Moses is forever associated with the dramatic encounters he had with the pharaoh of Egypt during which Moses declared God's demand that the Hebrew people who had been held in slavery for 430 years should be set free. The physical liberation of a long-oppressed people is at the heart of the story of Moses. You see, Exodus is not just the name of a book in the Bible. Exodus is the story of a man who spoke God's truth to earthly political power. Exodus is where God demonstrates that hard-hearted and "stiff-necked" rulers are no match for God's power, God's plan, and God's intentions for the people through whom God has chosen to work in the world.

Exodus is the term that describes how God used Moses to bring people from slavery to freedom. Exodus is the event in the twelfth century BCE that gave hope and inspiration to African American slaves in the nineteenth century CE as indicated by the lyrics in the song "Go Down Moses."[1]

In fact, it seems clear that over the years the story of Moses has been inseparably linked to the struggle for human freedom from slavery and oppression of every form and touching upon every human group. This was the sole mission given to Moses by God at the burning bush, to go back to Egypt and to tell Pharaoh to let the Hebrew people go free.

"Let my people go" is the heart of what Moses declared to Pharaoh. What will be argued in this chapter is that the making of a preacher is inseparably and inescapably linked to the content of the message delivered by Moses to Pharaoh. The message of liberation from all forms of bondage and oppression should be incorporated in the sermon content of twenty-first-century preachers, whether the issue involves oppression due to race, ethnicity, gender, sexual orientation, religious affiliation, disabilities, age, income level, or region of the country or the world. Preachers of the gospel must always stand with and speak up for those whom Jesus referred to in Matthew 25:44 (NIV) as "the least of these." Just as Moses spoke truth to power before the pharaoh of Egypt, so must twenty-first-century preachers be prepared to speak truth to power in today's world.

The story of Moses being sent before Pharaoh to demand freedom for the Hebrew people has taken on a special meaning within African American religious communities. Part of its popularity is certainly linked to the fact that nineteenth-century African Americans being held in slavery in the United States appropriated the story of Moses leading the Hebrew people out of slavery in Egypt as a hope that God might someday lead them on their own exodus from slavery in this country. So closely linked are Moses and the exodus from Egypt to the African American struggle for freedom in this country that Harriet Tubman, who was a leader in the Underground Railroad that brought hundreds of slaves into freedom in various northern states and in Canada, came to be known as the Moses of her people.[2]

The term "Black Moses" was also assigned to Marcus Garvey, the Jamaican-born Pan-Africanist who in 1919 to 1920 announced that he was going to lead a massive back-to-Africa movement that promised to deliver African Americans from perpetual second-class status in the United States by establishing a black homeland on the African continent.³ Garvey created the Universal Negro Improvement Association, whose message was that people of African ancestry all over the world were the objects of scorn and oppression. Whether in the United States, Canada, the nations of Europe, or the nations of the Caribbean, the problem was the same and so was the solution.

The story of Moses going down to tell Pharaoh to let the Hebrew people go free became the primary biblical source for black theology. Writing in *A Black Theology of Liberation*, James Cone focuses on the exodus as an indicator not only of what God did for Israel coming out of Egypt but also for what God's intentions are regarding all forms of human oppression. He begins with the biblical text of Exodus 19:4-5 that says, "You have seen what I did to the Egyptians, and how I bore you on eagle's wings and brought you to myself. Now therefore, if you obey my voice and keep my covenant, you shall be my treasured possession out of all the peoples." Cone continues by saying:

> God's call of this people is related to its oppressed condition and to God's own liberating activity already seen in the exodus. . . . By delivering this people from Egyptian bondage and inaugurating the covenant on the basis of that historical event, God is revealed as the God of the oppressed, involved in their history, liberating them from human bondage.⁴

Cone makes the link clearer between the story of Moses and the African American struggle for liberation from slavery and later forms of oppression. He states:

> The appearance of black theology on the American scene then is due primarily to the failure of white religionists to relate the gospel of Jesus to the pain of being black in a white racist society. It arises from the need of blacks to

liberate themselves from white oppressors. Black theology is a theology of liberation because it believes that the liberation of the black community is God's liberation.[5]

The making of a preacher as set forth in this book is a five-step process, and the matter of the content of sermons is the third step in that process. Using Moses as the model for how preachers are made, it must be concluded that his message of liberation from bondage for the Hebrew slaves must find its focus in all preaching in the twenty-first century. As Paul Tillich observed the rise of fascism in his native Germany, and as he observed the deafening silence coming from so many German pulpits at that time, he insisted that "preaching must be done with an awareness of the present moment."[6] Given all the social justice issues that confront and confound us today, it seems altogether unlikely that faithful preachers of the gospel can avoid touching upon some of those urgent matters in their sermons.

Do Not Try to Confront Pharaoh Every Sunday

While social justice issues must be incorporated in the preaching rotation, this does not imply or suggest that *every* sermon must focus on some matter of social justice. Faithful pastors and preachers will undoubtedly focus on a great many other themes in addition to matters of liberation and freedom from oppression. Cleophus LaRue reminds us when discussing the uniqueness of African American preaching, but with concerns that are applicable to preaching in all settings and styles, namely, that attention must be given to topics that fall under the rubrics of personal piety, care of the soul, corporate concerns, and maintenance of the institutional church.[7]

Some sermons will focus strictly on matters of individual spiritual formation, such as developing the disciplines of daily prayer, Bible study, charitable and philanthropic stewardship, and the importance of corporate worship (personal piety). Other sermons will seek to guide people through times of crisis, like the death of a loved one, a prolonged illness, the break-up of a marriage, the loss of a job, or the challenges of dealing with the aging process (care of the soul). Some sermons will deal with problems and challenges that are unique to a particular racial or cultural community (corporate concerns), and other sermons will focus on member responsibilities for the operation and programmatic work of their own local church (maintenance of the institutional church).

However, LaRue mentions a fifth category of concern that he calls social justice,[8] which must make its way into the preacher's sermon planning. This category of social justice is the one under which preachers can best think about how the content of the preaching of Moses before Pharaoh can inform their own preaching in the twenty-first century. As important as the other four categories of LaRue are when thinking about what makes for an effective pulpit ministry, there is no getting around this fifth category of social justice. Whether the problem at hand involves some unjust public policy, some unfair government practice, or some unreasonable denial of human rights such as affordable housing or health care, faithful preachers are the ones who are prepared to go before the power structures of this world and of their own respective communities and declare, "Let my people go." In short, preachers are not fully made until they have incorporated into their preaching God's demand for the liberation of oppressed people across this country and around the world.

Tell Old Pharaoh

At this point two important things are going on with the story of Moses that bear closer attention. The first involves how Moses spoke to Pharaoh. The second has to do with what Moses told Pharaoh he must do.

There is no mistaking what is going on in the first instance. God told Moses to "tell Pharaoh" (Exodus 6:11). Pharaohs, like all people with great power, are unaccustomed to being told to do anything. You may be able to plead with them, or beg or entreat them, or appeal to their mercy or benevolence. You can prostrate yourself before them like Mephibosheth bowed prostrate before David (2 Samuel 9:6-8). Perhaps you can cajole people in power with flattery to soften them up before you politely request something from them. Those are the approaches with which powerful people are quite familiar.

In the film *Django Unchained*, one slave pleads with an overseer who is about to whip another slave for some offense. He offers to take the beating that was about to be administered to the other slave, who happened to be his wife. He gets down on his knees and pleads with the overseer not to whip the woman, who is already being lashed. The overseer says to Django, "Boy, I like the way you beg."[9] That is the way people in power are accustomed to being approached. What they are not familiar with is anyone attempting to tell them to do something. What they are not familiar with is someone giving them an ultimatum of doing something, "or else." That approach could be a risky proposition when dealing with a person whose power may be exceeded only by their vanity. Yet, that is exactly what God instructed Moses to do: "Tell old Pharaoh to let my people go."

Repeatedly, Pharaoh tries to ignore, then negotiate, and then seek some compromise regarding what he is being told by Moses that he must do. Moses does not back up or lighten up his message. He keeps telling Pharaoh what to do to avoid feeling the wrath and power of a God whom Pharaoh does not believe in and will not obey. When God refers to Pharaoh as having a hard heart and a stiff neck, the resistance in Pharaoh's response is not just to what Moses is saying to him. The issue is how Moses is saying it. Standing in the royal palace, before the assembled members of the Egyptian royal court, being spoken to by someone who had spent the last forty years as a shepherd, the pharaoh of Egypt (who was believed to be a living god) is being told to do something: Let my people go.

In *Be My Witness*, I make the case for preachers engaging in something called "bold speech" based upon the Greek word *parrhesia*.[10] The American philosopher Cornel West defines *parrhesia* as "speaking the truth boldly and freely without any regard for the speaker's safety and security."[11] Bold speech is precisely what Moses was engaging in when he told Pharaoh to let the Hebrew people go free. Bold speech is precisely what preachers in the twenty-first century must engage in if we are to make any progress in the face of the numerous pressing issues that confront the church, the nation, and the world in this generation.

Lessons from Obama's Second Inaugural Address

One way to think about topics in the twenty-first century where preachers need to engage in bold speech or *parrhesia* is to reflect on a line that was spoken by President Barack Obama in his second inaugural address in 2013. While referring to three struggles for human rights and freedom and the equality of all persons, President Obama said the struggle extended "from Seneca Falls, to Selma, to Stonewall."[12] Seneca Falls was a reference to the struggle for women's rights, most especially the women's suffrage movement pursuing the right to vote, which began with the first Women's Convention held in Seneca Falls, New York, in 1848. Selma was a reference to the 1965 march from Selma to Montgomery, Alabama. That, too, was an effort to achieve voting rights, this time for African Americans. Stonewall was a reference to the resistance launched by LGBT persons following a police raid at the Stonewall night club in New York City in 1969, an event that gave birth to the gay rights movement in the United States.

What President Obama did was link together those three distinct human rights struggles that stretched over more than 120 years (from Seneca Falls in 1848 to Stonewall in 1969). Like Moses standing before Pharaoh crying out, "Let my people go," the leaders of these three human rights struggles were raising a similar cry. Whether the issue was a matter of gender, race and ethnicity, or gender identity and sexual orientation, it was bold speech without regard for the safety or security of the speakers who brought those freedom struggles to the attention of people in power, powerful people who were then, and may continue to this day, to be reluctant to act on what was being demanded.

Learning from Frederick Douglass

These three human rights movements reflected the approach to problem solving favored by Frederick Douglass, who was a leader in the abolitionist movement that sought to end human slavery in this country and around the world. In 1857, while speaking in Canandaigua, New York, outside of Rochester, Douglass said:

> **Power concedes nothing without a demand. It never has and it never will. Who would be free, themselves must strike the blow. If there is no struggle there is no progress. Those who profess to favor freedom and yet deprecate agitation are men who want crops without plowing up the ground; they want rain without thunder and lightning. They want the ocean without the roar of its many waters. This struggle may be a moral one, or it may be a physical one, and it may be both moral and physical, but it must be a struggle.**[13]

This was bold speech. This was *parrhesia*. This was a lesson on how to shape the content of a message that was intended to demand human rights. Every human rights struggle in this country has adopted the model of Frederick Douglass to boldly cry out, "Let my people go." A little-known fact about this speech by Douglass in 1857 is that it was delivered at an event called West Indies Emancipation Day, with special attention given to the nation of Haiti that had fought to win its independence from France in 1804. Thus, the call by Douglass for persons to demand further freedoms was spoken at an event that honored a physical, antislavery freedom struggle.

It must be noted that Frederick Douglass remained committed to the struggle for human rights virtually until his dying day. Just days before his death in 1895, a young African American male asked Douglass if he could offer any advice by which that young man could shape and guide his life. It is reported that Douglass stood up, gazed toward the heavens, and said, "Agitate! Agitate! Agitate!"[14] That is what Moses did before Pharaoh. That is what Elizabeth Cady Stanton and Susan B. Anthony did through the women's suffrage movement. That is what Martin Luther King Jr. and John Lewis and so many others were doing when they marched from Selma to Montgomery. That is what persons in the LGBT community have been doing ever since the Stonewall uprising.

The comedian and social critic Dick Gregory died while this book was being written. In one of his monologues, Gregory made the following observation: "If you put a load of dirty clothes in a washing machine and then remove the agitator, all you will have at the end of the wash cycle are wet, dirty clothes."[15]

These topics of social justice and the unjust policies and practices that predated these protests must be a regular part of the preaching rotation. There must be those Sundays and those other occasions when the goal of the preacher and the sermon and the Holy Spirit is to agitate, agitate, agitate! Call it a passion for social justice. Call it righteous indignation. Call it prophetic fervor. Call it anything you want so long as you include these issues in your preaching rotation.

Seneca Falls

These three human rights movements are not just about the headline-grabbing issues that one might immediately focus upon. Rather, each one of them opens the door to a host of related challenges and concerns that similarly require some bold speech, some *parrhesia* to resolve them. For instance, Seneca Falls opens the door to equal pay for equal work for women. It reminds us of the ongoing sexual exploitation of women, including the detestable comments by Donald Trump in an *Access Hollywood* interview in which he boasted about his celebrity status allowing him to grab women by their genitals. It reminds us of the long list of names from Bill Cosby, to the Hollywood film producer Harvey Weinstein, to Mark Halperin, who was the executive editor of *Newsweek*, to Matt Lauer, who was a long-time presence on NBC's *Today Show*, all of whom been accused of sexual exploitation. It reminds us of Judge Roy Moore of Alabama, who lost his bid for a seat in the US Senate due in part to the multiple accusations of his abuse of teenage girls when he was an adult male in his thirties. It reminds us of Al Franken, a former US Senator from Minnesota. It reminds us of Bill O'Reilly of Fox News, Charlie Rose of PBS, of movie stars like Dustin Hoffman and Kevin Spacey. It reminds us of the "Me Too Movement," where women are stepping forward to tell their stories of sexual abuse and sexual violence.

Seneca Falls calls to mind those invisible glass ceilings that prevent women from rising as high at work and in society as their talents can and should take them. Seneca Falls reminds us that in the church as well as in the broader society the gifts and skills of women are often left untapped solely on the grounds of their gender. Many men and women have come to believe, based upon two Pauline texts found in 1 Corinthians 14 and 1 Timothy 2, that women are forever prohibited not just from preaching but even from speaking in their local churches. I have argued at length against this idea of women being limited in any way in the life of the church from the pulpit to the pew.[16]

It is amazing to think that persons who have cast their votes for women to serve in elective offices ranging from the governor of a state, to a member of the US Congress, to president of the United States, should at the same time believe that those same women they voted for would not be welcomed to address their congregation while standing in the pulpit. Women can be astronauts who pilot a space shuttle up to the international space station, but they would not be similarly affirmed if they felt called to a second career in ministry. Women can be entrusted with the role of police officers, district attorneys, defense lawyers, even associate justices of the United States Supreme Court. However, in many churches and within many entire denominations they cannot and will not be entrusted with the interpretation of biblical teachings.

I was present at a black Baptist denominational gathering at which a male preacher stated in his sermon that if his wife announced to him that the Lord had also called her to be a preacher then their next stop would be divorce court. His wife was seated in the front row when this was stated. The look on her face when the preacher made that statement led everyone present to believe that he was continuing in public a conversation they had already begun in private. Seneca Falls is not just about Elizabeth Cady Stanton or Susan B. Anthony or the nineteenth-century suffrage movement. It opens the doors for bold speech, for *parrhesia* about the human rights and the equal rights of women in all aspects of American society both inside the church and beyond.

As I was writing these comments, I saw a line on CNN reporting that in the White House in 2017 women receive 80 cents for every dollar earned by men engaged in the exact same job. In thinking about the ongoing struggle for women's rights in the United States and around the world, I am reminded of the famous quote by Senator Ted Kennedy, who said in his eulogy for his brother Robert Kennedy, "The work goes on, the cause endures, the hope still lives, and the dream shall never die."[17]

Selma

Selma may be a chapter in the civil rights movement of the 1960s, but it has amazing relevance to life in the twenty-first century. Selma speaks against the outrageous "birther movement" launched by now-President Donald Trump that President Barack Obama was not born in the United States and thus was not qualified to serve in the office to which he was twice elected by the American people. It similarly points to Senator Mitch McConnell of Kentucky, who brazenly stated that "his number-one goal was to make sure that Barack Obama was a one-term president."[18] Selma opens the door to Black Lives Matter and the scandal of police officers shooting unarmed and non-threatening African American men, women, and children. It reminds us of Michael Brown, Freddie Gray, Philando Castile, Trayvon Martin, Tamir Rice, Sandra Bland, Walter Scott, Samuel Dubose, Eric Garner, Anthony Lamar Smith, Anton Rose and others who died at the hands of or in the custody of police officers.

Selma reminds us of Michelle Alexander's research about the staggering rate of arrest, conviction, and incarceration of African American and Hispanic people in this country.[19] When taken together, Seneca Falls and Selma are reminders of the poverty that works to limit the opportunities of single mothers and African Americans working every day on low-wage jobs.[20] It points to stunning rates of neighborhood seg-regation in cities across America as demonstrated in the book *Evicted,* by Matthew Desmond, which looks exclusively at the northern city of Milwaukee, Wisconsin.[21] Given that the driving factor for the Selma-to-Montgomery march of 1965 was gaining voting rights for African Americans in Alabama, it is amazing to consider that chief among the political talking points of many elected officials in 2018 is how to suppress, not increase, the voting rights of many Americans.[22]

Selma reminds us of the rise of white supremacist orga-nizations, often under the rubric of "the alt right," and their presence inside the White House in the person of an advisor to President Trump who had previously been the editor of Breitbart News, which has been "an online haven for white nationalists."[23] It requires that we pay close attention to the National Policy Network and Richard B. Spencer, whom the Southern Poverty Law Center calls "one of the country's most successful young white nationalist leaders—a suit-and-tie version of the white supremacists of old, a kind of profes-sional racist in khakis."[24] Preachers have much to talk about, to focus on, to direct their bold speech when they think about the implications of Selma in the twenty-first century.

Selma reminds us of the tragic events in Charlottesville, Virginia, in the summer of 2017, when hundreds of white men carried torchlights, Confederate flags, and swastikas, and chanted the Nazi slogan of "blood and soil." It reminds us of Heather Heyer, a white woman who was killed in Char-lottesville[25] when a twenty-year old white supremacist named James Alex Fields Jr. drove his car into a group of people who were protesting the presence of the Ku Klux Klan in their community.[26] Selma also reminds us of the comments of President Donald Trump, who stated that there was violence "on both sides" and very fine people "on both sides."[27] Remarkably, he repeated his view on September 14, 2017, thus equating the neo-Nazis and white supremacists with the peaceful protesters who had gathered to oppose a message of hatred and intolerance.[28]

Preaching that confronts the issues of racism has never been more relevant or more urgent. Such preaching must address the presumptions of white supremacy, the resegregation of schools and neighborhoods, threats to voting rights for African Americans, police conduct with unarmed black motorists, and the election of Donald Trump, who seems intent on undoing anything and everything established by Barack Obama, whose citizenship Trump questioned publicly for eight years without a shred of evidence. He finally had to acknowledge that he had been wrong when, during the 2016 presidential campaign, he made a five-second statement that was not accompanied by an apology.[29]

Stonewall

Stonewall may be the most challenging arena for some people to enter because they have not sorted out their own feelings on the question of equal rights for LGBT people. Or perhaps they *have* sorted out their feelings. Perhaps they have made up their minds about LGBT issues, and their conclusion is that Stonewall focuses less on the issue of human rights and more about a matter of human sinfulness. Since I have begun speaking about Stonewall and the struggle for human rights and equal rights for LGBT persons I have been told on more than one occasion that my views on this matter are contrary to the teachings of Scripture.

Often, the first Scripture mentioned is Leviticus 18:22 (NIV), which says, "Do not have sexual relations with a man as one does with a woman; that is detestable." Romans 1:26-27 is the other text I hear being used to make the case that LGBT issues are more about human sin than they are about human rights. That passage says, in part, "Because of this God gave them over to shameful lusts. Even their women exchanged natural sexual relations for unnatural ones. In the same way, the men also abandoned natural relations with women and were inflamed with lust for one another" (NIV). Some may even extend their argument to include 1 Corinthians 6:9-10 (NIV), which says, "Neither the sexually immoral nor idolaters nor adulterers nor men who have sex with men nor thieves nor the greedy nor drunkards nor slanderers nor swindlers will inherit the kingdom of God."

I had a shocking conversation at the biennial convention of the American Baptist Churches USA in Portland, Oregon, with a person who was deeply committed to issues of racial equality but who was unabashedly focused on 1 Corinthians 6—at least the part that dealt with men having sex with other men. This person seemed far less interested in the rest of the behaviors mentioned in that passage: thieves, the greedy, drunkards, slanderers, and swindlers. For this person, the whole focus of the passage was on human sexual conduct, with far more ferocity on same-sex behavior than on adultery.

There was no subtlety to the person's position. There was no openness to the ongoing discussion about whether sexuality is as much a matter of biology as it is about a chosen behavior. "All homosexuals are going to be banned from the kingdom of God." Moreover, I was criticized for suggesting anything to the contrary. This person boasted about holding views that reflected true Christian holiness. I guess that means that my views reflected my acceptance of what this person believed to be human sinfulness.

That encounter reflected what I always find so amazing about many people who approach LGBT issues from the position of sinfulness. They are unfailingly selective in the verses or portions of verse in Scripture they are reading. Such persons can be outraged and outspoken about same-sex activity, which is referenced in all three of the verses mentioned above. However, they are generally tolerant of, mute about, or wholly disinterested in other behaviors that either appear elsewhere in Leviticus or in the verses immediately after Romans 1:27 and 1 Corinthians 6:9. If they kept reading Paul in the two passages they love to quote, they would encounter thieves, the greedy, drunkards, slanderers, and swindlers, who are similarly being barred from the kingdom of God. They would discover Paul's additional references to envy, murder, strife, deceit, malice, gossip, arrogance, boastfulness, as well as a lack of fidelity and love and mercy. Surely all of these matters should be the object of bold speech or *parrhesia*, since they all appear in Romans 1 and 1 Corinthians 6.

There can be little doubt that all our churches have members who are involved in all the behaviors and attitudes mentioned by Paul in these two passages. But it is also true that very little sermon time is devoted to theft, gossip, slander, jealousy, boastfulness, envy, arrogance, or deceit. What is even more amazing is to hear preachers who are publicly known for their acts of adultery displaying righteous indignation on the single issue of same-sex activity. There are preachers who have no shortage of boastfulness or arrogance about the success of their own ministry. There is also no shortage of preachers who envy the successes and achievements of some of their clergy colleagues. Yet, they can look past all of that, which is so clearly present in Romans 1 and 1 Corinthians 6, and bring laser focus to the one behavior they want to vilify.

This is nothing short of homiletic hypocrisy, where preachers are willing to engage in bold speech on one topic mentioned by Paul which involves a small percentage of their listening audience, while saying little or nothing at all about the other matters mentioned by Paul in the same verses of Scripture, behaviors which very likely affect everyone present including the preacher. One of the reasons many people are walking away from the church today is because they are walking away from this kind of judgmentalism and hypocrisy and intolerance of LGBT people.[30]

The same point could be made about Leviticus 18:22. There are many more practices to be considered in that tenth-century BCE holiness code to which modern readers could hold themselves accountable. Leviticus calls upon husbands to abstain from sexual contact with their wives during women's menstrual cycle (15:19-33). I have yet to hear a sermon about that, and that is also in Leviticus 18. I wonder how many people who point to Leviticus as the basis of their condemnation of same-sex relationships also abstain from eating shell fish (11:10) or wearing clothing made of more than one fabric (19:19). You cannot wear a silk-and-wool suit to Red Lobster where you enjoy lobster or crab or shrimp, and use that meal as an occasion to condemn the LGBT community. Leviticus 19:28 prohibits putting a tattoo on one's body. In this age of tattoos all over people's bodies, I have yet to hear a sermon on that.

There is a great danger attached to people who use the Bible selectively, only referencing the verses that seem to support the issues they choose to highlight, while blatantly ignoring verses that get in the way of the bigoted views they are attempting to offer up as gospel truth. This selective use of Scripture to justify something that is otherwise corrupt or unintended by the Scriptures occurred when US Attorney General Jeff Sessions attempted to justify the cruel practice of separating parents from their children at the border with Mexico by quoting Romans 13.[31] That verse calls on people to "Be subject to the governing authorities, for there is no authority except that which God has established." Of course, that was the same verse that slave masters in the 19th century used to justify slavery, that the Nazis used to justify the Holocaust, and that the white-minority government of South Africa used to justify apartheid.[32]

Confession: My Own Sinful Past

I must confess that I was not always where I am today on the matter of LGBT rights. I was born into a generation and grew up in a time and place where LGBT persons felt it necessary to keep their sexuality as a closely kept secret for fear of harassment from those whom they considered their friends. The anxiety was even worse when it came to those they did not know as well. I was well into college in the 1960s before I encountered openly LGBT persons who were both in the student body and on the faculty. Getting to know them caused me to reconsider the prejudices I had been carrying for so many years. I was in my seminary years in the 1970s before I was aided in shaping the biblical and theological grounds upon which my advocacy for the rights of LGBT persons could be articulated.

My conversion was not a Damascus Road experience when I was suddenly and dramatically transformed in the twinkling of an eye. Mine was a process of soul searching, Bible study, long hours of conversation, and finally developing close friendships with persons in the LGBT community. Today, those within the LGBT community will find no better friend or fiercer advocate. Similarly, those who seek to insult or assault or in any way place limits on the full and equal rights of LGBT persons will find no fiercer critic.

There is one moment in particular in my spiritual journey on LGBT issues that causes me continued pain, regret, and embarrassment. I was the preacher on Mother's Day at Abyssinian Baptist Church in New York City, where I was a member of the ministerial staff. At the wise old age of twenty-six, I decided to use that special day in the life of most black Baptist churches to intentionally pick a fight with gay men who were members of that church. I suggested that Mother's Day was a clear reminder of the differences between those persons who were women and those who only pretended or acted as if they were. Gay men could not share with women in the act of giving birth to children. Full of as much righteous indignation as I could muster, I used a sacred occasion to engage in a sinful assault on a group of people who were never given any opportunity to respond to my message.

Needless to say, that sermon created an uproar throughout the congregation. Later that evening a group of church members met and were preparing to demand that I be fired from my position. They made that demand of the senior pastor, Dr. Samuel DeWitt Proctor, the next day. Dr. Proctor had not been present that Sunday, having entrusted the pulpit to me, and now he was being called upon to acknowledge the crude analogy I had made in his absence. There is no doubt in my mind that he would never have done such a thing, and he was bitterly disappointed that I had done so before a gathered congregation of more than twenty-five hundred worshippers. He told those who asked that I be fired that he would not do so, choosing instead to turn that occasion into a teachable moment. He spoke with me at great length about "selective outrage" over the practices in which I did not engage, while saying nothing about the practices clearly set forth in Scripture in which he knew I regularly engaged.

To my eternal shame, I did in my own ministry the very things I now plead with other preachers not to do; I focused on one behavior mentioned in Scripture while ignoring or overlooking the many other practices, behaviors, and attitudes that are usually found in the same verses(s) that follow the references to matters of same-sex activity. We do need bold speech on the related issues of LGBT human rights. However, that bold speech must be directed less to the people in the pews and more to the people standing in the pulpit whose sermons on this matter are far more Pharisaic than they are prophetic! More often than not, it is we who preach who must be educated, challenged, and transformed in our own thinking as a first step toward *parrhesia* on matters dealing with Stonewall.

What Preaching Content Comes with Stonewall?

Perhaps more than either Seneca Falls or Selma, Stonewall points to a series of current concerns about which the twenty-first-century pulpit cannot be silent and should not approach solely based on a smug self-righteousness. Stonewall raises the question of marriage equality and the enjoyment of certain family rights that heterosexual married couples take for granted. Stonewall is a reminder that Black Lives Matter began in reaction to the frequent deaths of black transgender women. Stonewall reminds many people that their anti-gay views can suddenly and dramatically be challenged if not changed altogether when their own child "comes out" as being gay. Stonewall is at the heart of a current sociopolitical debate that involves whether business owners and service providers can deny their services to same-sex couples (wedding cakes, photo and video services, limousine services, banquet halls) because the owner of those services objects to same-sex couples on religious grounds.

Stonewall points to the recent decision by President Donald Trump to unilaterally ban transgender persons from any role within the armed forces of the United States. This is even though more than sixty-six hundred transgender persons have been openly living and bravely fighting and dying in this country's wars in both Iraq and Afghanistan for years.[33] Aaron Belkin, who is the director of the Palm Center which advocates for transgender troops, described Trump's actions by saying, "What happened is the commander-in-chief ordered a purge of transgender troops."[34]

It is not fair to expect that the only voices addressing these issues are those in the LGBT community who are advocating for themselves. There is another letter in the LGBTQIA term, and that is the letter A that stands for Allies, though I sometimes use the term "advocates." Allies or advocates of the LGBT community are not gay or lesbian, bisexual, or transgender themselves. Rather, they are persons who reject the notion that any person ought to be denied any human right or is deserving of any form of discrimination solely because of their gender identity or sexual orientation. Is the only option the church holds out to the LGBT community that they repent of their sins and come back to a "normal heterosexual lifestyle"? Surely, heterosexuals who suffer with more than a 50 percent divorce rate in their marriages, and who are at the heart of domestic abuse and the brutalization of women, should walk more softly on this ground. The hypocrisy of the church concerning LGBT issues is not unlike the hypocrisy of the Roman Catholic Church and the pedophilia that infected the ranks of what the world presumed was a celibate priesthood.

How Can Our Stonewall Discussion Begin?

How can churches begin a discussion about LGBT-related issues? How can churches see the importance of Stonewall no less than the struggles associated with Seneca Falls and Selma? It can begin with doing better biblical exegesis that studies the texts mentioned above through the lens of twenty-first-century sensibilities. We have concluded in the last several centuries that we will not stone women caught in adultery, even though the people of ancient Israel did exactly that. We have decided not to endorse the practice of human slavery, even though Paul himself not only failed to condemn that practice but also suggested guidelines that both slaves and slave owners should observe. As mentioned above, if people insist on approaching the issue of homosexuality strictly from the position of sin and judgment, then they must be as forceful in their condemnation regarding the other behaviors found throughout Leviticus and within Romans 1 and 1 Corinthians 6.

The discussion can include whether persons in the LGBT community are there by behavioral choice or by biological predisposition. The discussion can include whether all persons deserve the human rights protections our society affords to every citizen. The discussion can consider the fact that LGBT persons are not strangers in some faraway setting. Instead, they are among our closest friends, members of our own family. They are leaders in our civic and political life, and they are members of our nation's armed forces and our communities' first responders who risk their lives every day to keep us safe.

In *The Making of the Sermon*, Robert McCracken mentions four possible outcomes for every sermon.[35] Those outcomes are:

1. To kindle the mind, which involves enabling people to think deeply about a topic on which there is not yet broad agreement in the church or in society.

2. To energize the will, which involves people taking some necessary action in defense of or in response to some issue concerning which they are now persuaded.

3. To disturb the conscience, which is to encourage people to repent of the thoughts, attitudes, values, and past practices which they have now become convinced are ungodly and out of step with the mind of Christ.

4. To stir the heart, which occurs when people are reminded that God's grace is sufficient, God's love is inclusive, and God's church is a safe place for all God's people no matter their age, gender, ethnicity or race, their handicaps, or their sexual orientation.

It may be that the best way for preachers to begin a discussion of LGBT-related issues is by using McCracken's first outcome objective, kindle the mind. It is unlikely that many people will be argued out of a deeply held position unless they are presented with some facts and points of view that they can think about long after the sermon is over. "Kindle the mind" is an invitation to think about what has been said and to begin considering one's own views in light of this new information. While there is likely room for energizing the will and for disturbing the conscience later, it would probably be best if preachers started by addressing the minds of their listeners, and then work their way to their heart.

Here I Stand, I Can Do No Other

When called before the Diet of Worms in 1521 to give an account for the views he held that seemed out of line with sixteenth-century Roman Catholic theology and practice, Martin Luther refused to recant his views. Instead, tradition tells us that he declared, "Here I stand, I can do no other."[36] Luther seemed reconciled to the fact that he would not be able to convince or convert those who were opposed to his views on the authority of Scripture, the nature of papal authority, or the idea of salvation by faith and not by works. Nevertheless, he was determined to remain true to his own convictions, no matter how unpopular they were with some of his contemporary church leaders. As it happened, Luther was eventually excommunicated from the Roman Catholic Church, the worst outcome any member of that church could possibly endure. Luther knew that eventuality was possible when he took his stand, but conscience won out over conformity to the status quo. Thus, he declared, "Here I stand, I can do no other."

The example of Martin Luther has been replicated by the leaders of every movement being discussed here. Each of them decided that it was time to take a stand, no matter how unpopular their views and actions might prove to be. This is the heart of bold speech or *parrhesia*, speech that is delivered without regard to the safety and security of the speaker. That was true for Elizabeth Cady Stanton and Susan B. Anthony on the issues that emerged from Seneca Falls. In fact, in 1872 Susan B. Anthony was arrested when she attempted to vote in Rochester, New York. It was true for Rosa Parks, Medgar Evers, Fannie Lou Hamer, and Martin Luther King Jr. on the issues that revolved around Selma.

It was true for Harvey Milk when he became the openly gay mayor of San Francisco. It was true for Bayard Rustin, the architect of the 1963 March on Washington who lived as an openly gay male. The same can be said of the author James Baldwin, the news anchors Don Lemon and Anderson Cooper both of CNN and Rachel Maddow of MSNBC. The decision by some to reveal their sexual orientation has made it easier for others to make the same announcement concerning themselves. As regards Seneca Falls, Selma, and Stonewall, people are saying to themselves and to the world, "Here I stand."

In the case of each of those human rights struggles, many people in the country were content with an unjust status quo on issues of gender and race. That opposition did not stop those human rights advocates who were determined to take a stand for a more inclusive society, often at great personal risk. Medgar Evers, the leader of the Mississippi state chapter of the NAACP, had earlier belonged to a segregated military unit that was a part of the D-Day invasion force on the beaches of Normandy, France, that began on June 6, 1944.[37] However, he would be shot in the back in Jackson, Mississippi, in 1963 because he was agitating for the right to vote in the country for which he had risked his life. He knew his life was in danger, but he took his stand.

These examples call to mind the words of Nelson Mandela spoken just before he began serving what ended up being a twenty-seven-year prison sentence in South Africa. He said:

> **During my life, I have dedicated myself to this struggle of the African people. I have fought against white domination, and I have fought against black domination. I have cherished the ideal of a democratic and free society in which all persons live together in harmony and with equal opportunities. It is an ideal which I hope to live for and achieve. But if needs be, it is an ideal for which I am prepared to die.**[38]

The focus of the final chapter of this book is on the consequences that can occur when preachers engage in bold speech such as was demonstrated by Moses. I will return to this topic when we get to that point. For the time being, preachers need to consider their willingness to engage in bold speech or *parrhesia*. A willingness to preach outside the biblical, cultural, political, and even denominational comfort zone of most people in the pulpit and in the pew is part of what is involved in the making of a preacher.

■ ■ ■

Notes

1. James Weldon Johnson and J. Rosamond Johnson, *The Book of American Negro Spirituals*, vol. 1 (New York: Viking, 1953), 51.
2. Earl Conrad, *A Biography of Harriet Tubman* (New York: Paul Erikkson, 1943), 47.
3. Edmund David Cronon, *Black Moses: The Story of Marcus Garvey and the Universal Negro Improvement Association* (Madison: University of Wisconsin Press, 1969), 4, 53–59.
4. James H. Cone, *A Black Theology of Liberation* (Maryknoll, NY: Orbis Books, 1986), 2.
5. Ibid., 4–5.
6. Paul Tillich, quoted in Karl Barth, *The Preaching of the Gospel* (Philadelphia: Westminster Press, 1963), 54.
7. Cleophus J. LaRue, *The Heart of Black Preaching* (Louisville, KY: Westminster/John Knox, 2000), 21–25.
8. Ibid., 23.
9. *Django Unchained*, Columbia Pictures, 2013.
10. Marvin A. McMickle, *Be My Witness* (Valley Forge, PA: Judson Press, 2016), 101.
11. Cornel West with Christa Buschendorf, *Black Prophetic Fire* (Boston: Beacon Press, 2014), 112.
12. Barack Obama, second inaugural address, January 20, 2013.
13. Frederick Douglass, "If There Is No Struggle There Is No Progress," in *The Voice of Black America: Major Speeches by Negroes in the United*

States 1797–1971, ed. Philip Foner (New York: Simon and Schuster, 1972), 197–203.

14. John Stauffer, *Giants: The Parallel Lives of Frederick Douglass and Abraham Lincoln* (New York: Twelve/12, 2008), 314.

15. Bryan Alexander, "Dick Gregory Shattered the Mold On Stage and Off," *USA Today*, August 21, 2017, 6B.

16. Marvin A. McMickle, "In the Footsteps of Phoebe," in *Deacons in Today's Black Baptist Church* (Valley Forge: Judson Press, 2010), 76–90; Marvin A. McMickle, *Challenging Gender Discrimination in the Church* (Valley Forge, PA: ABCUSA Ministers Council, 2011).

17. Huma Kahn, "Ted Kennedy Quotes: In His Own Words," April 26, 2009, ABC News, https://abcnews.go.com/Politics/TedKennedy/story?id=8417543.

18. Glenn Kessler, "When Did McConnell Say He Wanted to Make Obama a 'One-Term President'?" *The Washington Post*, September 25, 2012, https://www.washingtonpost.com/blogs/fact-checker/post/when-did-mcconnell-say-he-wanted-to-make-obama-a-one-term-president/2012/09/24/79fd5cd8-0696-11e2-afff-d6c7f20a83bf_blog.html?utm_term=.fff152a58ccb.

19. Michelle Alexander, *The New Jim Crow: Mass Incarceration in the Age of Colorblindness* (New York: The New Press, 2012).

20. David Rolf, *The Fight for $15: The Right Wage for a Working America* (New York: The New Press, 2016).

21. Matthew Desmond, *Evicted: Poverty and Profit in the American City* (New York: Crown, 2016).

22. Marvin A. McMickle, "The Real Issue Is Voter Suppression," *Democrat and Chronicle*, blog, February 27, 2017, https://www.democratandchronicle.com/story/news/local/blogs/unite/2017/01/27/real-issue-voter-suppression/97156394/.

23. Sarah Posner, "How Donald Trump's New Campaign Chief Created an Online Haven for White Nationalists," *Mother Jones*, August 22, 2016, https://www.motherjones.com/politics/2016/08/stephen-bannon-donald-trump-alt-right-breitbart-news/.

24. Southern Poverty Law Center, "Richard Bertrand Spencer," https://www.splcenter.org/fighting-hate/extremist-files/individual/richard-bertrand-spencer-0.

25. "Charlottesville Mourns Woman Killed in a Rally That Turned Violent," *The Washington Post*, August 16, 2017, https://www.washingtonpost.com/lifestyle/kidspost/charlottesville-mourns-woman-killed-in-rally-that-turned-violent/2017/08/16/29975362-8296-11e7-902a-2a9f2d808496_story.html?utm_term=.16b0be097353.

26. Ibid.; Marvin A. McMickle, "Trump Creates Climate for Hatred to Grow," *Democrat and Chronicle*, August 20, 2017, 31A, https://www.democratandchronicle.com/story/opinion/guest-column/2017/08/14/marvin-mcmickle-trump-charlottesville/564343001/.

27. Michael D. Shear and Maggie Haberman, "Trump Defends Initial Remarks on Charlottesville; Again Blames 'Both Sides,'" August 15,

2017, https://www.nytimes.com/2017/08/15/us/politics/trump-press-conference-charlottesville.html.

28. Tamara Keith, "President Trump Stands by Original Charlottesville Remarks," NPR, September 14, 2017, https://www.npr.org/2017/09/14/551069462/president-trump-stands-by-original-charlottesville-remarks.

29. Stephen Collinson and Jeremy Diamond, "Trump Finally Admits It: 'President Barack Obama Was Born in the United States,'" CNN, September 16, 2016, https://www.cnn.com/2016/09/15/politics/donald-trump-obama-birther-united-states/index.html.

30. See David Kinnamen and Gabe Lyons, *Unchristian: What a New Generation Really Thinks about Christianity . . . and Why It Matters* (Grand Rapids, MI: Baker Books, 2007).

31. Julie Jacobs, "Session's Use of Bible Passage to Defend Immigration Policy Draws Ire," NewYorkTimes.com, June 15, 2018.

32. Jennifer Rubin, "Leave the Bible out of it, child separation is not 'Christian'," TheWashingtonPost.com, June 15, 2018.

33. Tom Vander Brook, "Trump Takes on Gender Policy," *USA Today*, July 26, 2017, B1–2.

34. Ibid., B2.

35. Robert McCracken, *The Making of the Sermon* (New York: Harper and Row, 1956), 18.

36. Roland Bainton, *Christendom*, vol. 2 (New York: Harper Torchbooks, 1964), 21.

37. Barbara Maranzani, "Seven Things You Should Know about Medgar Evers," History Stories, The History Channel, June 11, 2013, https://www.history.com/news/7-things-you-should-know-about-medgar-evers.

38. Nelson Mandela, *Long Walk to Freedom: The Autobiography of Nelson Mandela* (New York: Little, Brown, 1994), 368.

Chapter 6

Hatred and Bigotry Are Not Relics of a Distant Past

If liberty can be denied to anyone, it could eventually be denied
to you! —Abraham Lincoln

Injustice anywhere is a threat to justice everywhere.
—Martin Luther King Jr.

■ ■ ■

It must be clear that the issues flowing from Seneca Falls,
Selma, and Stonewall are as current as this morning's
newspapers. In the July 7, 2017, edition of *USA Today*,
all three of these topics were front and center. First, there
was a story about a Harvard University club called The Fox
that revoked the membership of nine female members on the
sole grounds of gender, asserting that the club was open only
to male members. That decision came after women had been
accepted into the club in 2015. However, alumni members
of that club who longed for the all-male environs that had
defined that club in years past overruled the members in the
current student body. Only one alumnus spoke against that
decision: Douglas Sears, who was president of the graduate
board in 2015 when the decision to admit women was approved. Sears stated, "Some folks certainly know to get on
the wrong side of history."[1] Many people are on the wrong
side of history as far as the equal worth and full human rights
of women.

In that same issue, Paul Raushenbush of Auburn Seminary
linked Selma and Stonewall in a letter to the editor of *USA*

Today. In talking about how some people have used the Bible to justify their views about the LGBT community, Raushenbush wrote, "One only need look back at the treatment of interracial couples to find sincere Christians citing biblical beliefs to legislate against the love shared between couples of different races."[2]

On the days before these articles in *USA Today*, two articles appeared in *The New York Times* that carried the issues of Selma into the twenty-first century. The first one was about the fact that, until 1967, interracial marriage was against the law in many states in this country.[3] The second article, from July 5, 2017, was about the increasing appearance of more and more nooses, the dreaded symbol of the lynch mob, frequently in the most unexpected places—at the United States Mint in Philadelphia, on the campus of the University of Maryland, at American University in Washington, DC, and even inside the National Museum of African American History and Culture.[4] Selma occurred in 1965, but racism is as fresh and vibrant as the repeated shootings of unarmed black men by police officers who are invariably acquitted if they are charged at all.

Issues related to Stonewall also appeared in the July 7, 2017, *USA Today*. An openly gay Justice Department lawyer expressed deep disappointment that President Trump chose not to issue a statement of support during Gay Pride Month in June 2017. It was pointed out that Trump had issued a statement in support of National Home Ownership Month, African American Music Appreciation Month, and Great Outdoors Month. In his speech at the 2016 Republican National Convention he had seemed to offer support to the LGBT community when he said, "As your president, I will do everything in my power to protect our LGBT citizens from the violence and oppression of a hateful ideology."[5] Those remarks were made in the aftermath of the terrorist attack on a nightclub in Orlando, Florida, that was popular with LGBT persons. However, less than one year later, President Trump chose silence during the entire month devoted to the LGBT community. In response to that intentional snub, Adam Chandler wrote, "The White House appears to be sending a painful message that we don't deserve the progress we've made, and that it's still not OK to be who we are."[6]

I have no doubt that not everyone will agree with the sentiments expressed in the previous chapter. Not everyone is in support of full rights for women in the church and in society. That is a fact. Not everyone is free from the centuries-long legacy of racial prejudice and discrimination against African Americans. That is also a fact. Similarly, not everyone is free from their view that LGBT issues are not about human rights but are simply and solely about human sinfulness. It is clear to me that many well-meaning people (Christians included) are not prepared to stand with those who are supportive of the issues surrounding Stonewall. They do not pause to consider the very real possibility that homosexual conduct may be a matter of biology and how a person has been constructed, rather than a matter of behavioral choice. The church and the broader society remain deeply divided on how to respond to LGBT persons.

Consider the conduct of two Roman Catholic Church leaders. Cardinal Joseph Tobin of Newark, New Jersey, welcomed gay and lesbian persons to a special Mass at the cathedral church. At that Mass he said, "I am your brother as a disciple of Jesus."[7] In that same article reference was made to Bishop Thomas Paprocki of Illinois, "who instructed priests not to offer Holy Communion or funeral rites to anyone engaged in a same-sex union unless they had given some sign of repentance before their death. . . . Many of the country's bishops linger somewhere between Tobin's welcome and Paprocki's warning."[8] That is another fact that must be understood.

A recent *New York Times* editorial pointed to the broad divide within the Roman Catholic Church on matters related to Stonewall. It focused on Cardinal Joseph Tobin of Newark, New Jersey, and Cardinal Timothy Dolan of New York City. The editorial makes the point that two cardinals, the second-highest ranking office in that communion after the office of the pope, residing on opposite sides of the Hudson River, appeal to two very different constituencies within the Roman Catholic Church in America.[9]

It is likely that both sides on this issue are defending their position by declaring, "Here I stand, I can do no other." Far be it from me to cast any negative judgment or condemnation on those who do not agree with the views that have been expressed here. All I can say at this point is that I see Seneca Falls, Selma, and Stonewall through the same lens, the lens employed by President Obama in 2013. All three of these movements were and continue to be legitimate struggles for full human rights. More importantly, all three of these human rights struggles must be part of the bold speech, the *parrhesia* of preachers in the twenty-first century. The ability to do so is part of what is entailed in the making of a preacher whose voice will have relevance in today's world. There is ample room for dissent on this topic, but there is no room for silence.

From Seneca Falls to Selma, to Stonewall, to Standing Rock

As I suggest in an issue of *Christian Citizen*, there is a fourth struggle for human rights that Obama might have included if he were giving his inaugural address in 2017: the struggle for human rights and environmental protections at the Standing Rock Indian Reservation outside of Bismarck, North Dakota.[10] That protest was going on at the very hour the 2017 inauguration was taking place in Washington, DC. At Standing Rock, the Lakota Sioux and thousands of their supporters were protesting the construction of an oil pipeline that would likely suffer an oil spill and endanger the water supply not only for their reservation but also for six neighboring states.

One of the leaders of that resistance movement is Father John Floberg, an Episcopal priest from nearby Bismarck, North Dakota, who has fearlessly and consistently engaged in bold speech, in *parrhesia* as he calls the nation's attention to this human and environmental injustice. Melanie Duguid May, a member of our faculty at Colgate Rochester Crozer Divinity School, was among the people who traveled to Standing Rock in 2017, just like people traveled to Selma in 1965. Later that same year of 2017, CRCDS invited Father John Floberg to be our commencement speaker, because we wanted our graduates to go into the world more keenly aware of the issues that relate to Seneca Falls, Selma, Stonewall, and Standing Rock.

I challenge preachers to consider the opportunities for bold speech that await them when they reflect upon these four human rights struggles: Seneca Falls and the rights of women; Selma and the rights of African Americans; Stonewall and the claims for full equality and equal opportunity for LGBT persons; Standing Rock and the nearly six-hundred-year history of the exploitation and near extermination of indigenous people throughout North, Central, and South America. Once again, this is not a call to address these topics every Sunday. However, it is a reminder that while a good pastor will address a wide range of other topics, a faithful pastor must address issues such as these on a regular basis.

Standing Rock

So, let us consider the fourth issue that could easily be added to the list offered by President Obama in his second inaugural address, and that is the issue related to the concerns expressed by Native Americans at the Standing Rock reservation. This issue involves those who have been protesting the building of the Dakota Access Pipeline that will carry crude oil from North Dakota, across the Missouri River, to a refinery and secondary pipeline in Illinois. It also involves the Keystone Pipeline that carries oil from Canada to the Gulf of Mexico. Those oil pipelines will pass through Native American ancestral burial grounds. They will also disrupt hunting and fishing rights for the Sioux Indians on that reservation who depend upon hunting and fishing for their survival. Most important of all, those two pipelines also run the risk of an oil spill that can pollute the water supply for the entire human and animal population of several neighboring states. In fact, there has already been a massive oil spill from the Keystone Pipeline. On November 16, 2017, 210,000 gallons of oil leaked from the pipeline in South Dakota.

The issue is further complicated by the fact that Standing Rock is private land owned by and for the benefit of the Lakota Sioux nation. Like so many agreements between Native

American groups and the US federal government, ownership rights lost out to corporate interests, and the pipeline was well underway until President Obama put a temporary freeze on the project until all possible environmental dangers could be identified and resolved.[11] The freeze by President Obama was lifted by President Trump, and the construction of the pipeline continues without the issues of ownership or environmental impact being resolved.

The bold speech opportunities for Christian preachers are easily apparent. It begins with the centuries-long exploitation and near extermination of Native Americans. I grew up in Chicago, a name which derives from an Indian word (*chicagoua*) for a garlic plant. I have lived in Cleveland, in the county of Cuyahoga, which is an Indian word for "crooked river." Not far away is Geauga County, which is a Seneca word that means "raccoon." Now I live in western New York, which still boasts of being home to the Seneca Nation. The famous Finger Lakes region has an Indian name for each of those lakes: Canandaigua, Keuka, Cayuga, Honeoye, Conesus, Onondaga, and Owasco, among others. Where are the people from whom those names were assigned? In truth, they were brutally and forcefully removed from their land to make room for earlier equivalents of the Dakota Access Pipeline. Had there been more bold speech by preachers in the nineteenth century, the history of Native Americans might look and read very differently.

In 2016 there was a nationwide discussion about changing the face on this nation's twenty-dollar bill. The face of Andrew Jackson currently appears on that currency, but two issues drove the decision to replace his image with that of Harriet Tubman. First, Andrew Jackson was a slaveholder. Second, it was President Andrew Jackson who authorized the 1830 Indian Removal Act that required all Native Americans living east of the Mississippi River to be forcibly relocated to the region that is now the state of Oklahoma.[12] The underlying reason for that forced removal was to allow for the expansion of growing cotton and the increase of slave labor that was essential to that enterprise. Because of the Indian

Removal Act, more than forty-six thousand Native Americans were relocated, and more than four thousand Cherokees died along what came to be called the Trail of Tears. Native Americans would eventually be moved onto government-sponsored reservations where today they experience staggering levels of alcoholism, depression, drug addiction, domestic violence, infant mortality, unemployment, and the highest rates of suicide and teen suicide in the United States.[13]

It must not be forgotten that on November 27, 2017, President Trump stood in front of a portrait of that same Andrew Jackson when he honored the surviving members of the Navajo Code Talkers who were instrumental in so many battles in the Pacific during World War II.[14] Those heroic Navajo servicemen were "dumbfounded that Trump used that occasion to once again refer to US Senator Elizabeth Warren as 'Pocahontas,' turning the name of an historic figure into a derogatory term."[15] Russell Begaye, president of the Navajo Nation, said, "All tribal nations still battle insensitive references to our people. The prejudice that Native Americans face is an unfortunate historical legacy."[16]

Thanks to the film *Windtalkers*, this country was made aware of the role that Navajo Indians played in World War II, especially in the Pacific region in the fight against Japan. Navajo Indians sent radio messages to and from the front lines of the battles using their native language, which the Japanese had never heard and could not translate.[17] Thanks to the film *Flags of Our Fathers*, the nation discovered that one of the US Marines who raised the American flag on Mount Suribachi on the island of Iwo Jima during World War II was a Pima Indian from Arizona named Ira Hamilton Hayes.[18]

There are 326 Indian reservations across the country. One of them, the Pine Ridge Reservation in South Dakota, has also been in the news recently. Because of a massive influx of drugs known as methamphetamines, that reservation, which is home to twenty thousand Oglala Lakota Sioux, has seen a spike in murders and homicides. As of 2016, the murder rate on that reservation has doubled over the previous year. This places one reservation on par with the deadliest US cities in terms of gun violence.[19] In accounting for this reality, one of the elders of that community stated, "The Federal government has an obligation to guarantee law and order on Indian land. It has failed to do so ever since treaty times."[20] Because Native Americans have been forced onto land that is far removed from the view of the rest of our society there seems to be little awareness of the problems that exist there. This is one of the great justice issues of the twenty-first century.

Cartoons and Caricatures

The problem facing Native Americans is further exacerbated because of the historic and ongoing use of Native Americans as mascots for various athletic teams—the Florida State Seminoles, Cleveland Indians, Washington Redskins, Kansas City Chiefs, Atlanta Braves, Chicago Blackhawks, and Golden State Warriors, just to name a few. People who would never tolerate seeing their ethnic group reduced to a stereotyped logo on the jersey of a sports team seem to have no problem cheering for teams that display those images. Imagine a team called the New York Negroes or the New Jersey Jews. Such a thing would be unthinkable and unacceptable for most people in this country. But otherwise-justice-minded people happily cheer for such teams and ignore the voices of Native Americans who continue to insist that such logo images are both degrading and dehumanizing.

Hearing a Kiowa Woman from Oklahoma

In July 2017 I had the privilege of hearing a sermon delivered by a woman named Rev. Kathy Longhat from the Kiowa people of Oklahoma. The occasion was the biennial luncheon gathering of the American Baptist Home Mission Societies meeting in Portland, Oregon. She was preceded to the podium by her cousin, who sang a prayer inviting God to open the hearts of all who were gathered that day, so they could receive the message that was to come. If ever there was a Moses moment, this was it. Rev. Longhat told us about her struggle to accept her call to the ministry. She shared how hard it was to gain her voice as a woman within her male-dominant culture. She made an impassioned appeal for justice and equal opportunity for the people that the United States has conveniently removed from view by herding them onto reservations where the hardships they face every day go unnoticed by those who never venture to those locations.

I was grateful for the chance to be exposed to Kathy Longhat and the message that she both spoke and embodied. I would imagine that most of the five or six hundred persons gathered for the event where she spoke had never heard a sermon delivered by a Native American woman who was a descendant of those who had survived the systematic removal and relocation of her tribe. This was no cartoon character, no mascot image on a sports uniform, and no alien presence in our midst. This was an American Baptist preacher bringing to our attention the voices, the hopes, and the challenges being faced by our Native American brothers and sisters.

Standing Rock and National Defense

Rev. Kathy Longhat is not the only member of the Kiowa people who bears mention at this point. In the new Ken Burns documentary on the war in Vietnam, mention is made of the number of Kiowa Indians who trained at Fort Sill in Oklahoma and were then sent to Vietnam. The documentary noted that as a percentage of their US population, more Kiowa people fought in Vietnam than did any other ethnic or racial group.

Surely, communities that have suffered and sacrificed so much in defense of this country (Native Americans and African Americans) should be shown the same respect and offered the same opportunities as persons of any other racial or ethnic group. When that proves not to be the case, it is time for some bold speech in defense of those who have literally defended us.

Our Preaching Content Should Follow the Example of Moses

The four human rights struggles represented by Seneca Falls, Selma, Stonewall, and Standing Rock provide a clear path for preachers who are willing to follow the example of Moses in advocating for freedom and equal opportunity for all of God's people. To be sure, there are other issues in this country and around the world that are as urgent and important as those listed above. The goal of this chapter is not to limit the human rights struggles that are deserving of our bold speech as preachers. Rather, the goal is to urge every preacher of every denomination, race, gender, and region to be attentive to and outspoken concerning any of the forms of oppression faced by people all over the world. That was at the heart of the story of Moses. An Egyptian prince, born Hebrew but raised in the palace of Pharaoh, becomes the leader of a freedom movement only after he was willing to care about suffering that did not directly affect his life.

Another Personal Confession

I confess that my insistence on the importance of bold speech from the pulpit on matters of social justice comes because of the influence of those who shaped my life and thought. My pulpit mentors were Martin Luther King Jr., William Augustus Jones Jr., Gardner C. Taylor, and Samuel DeWitt Proctor. My academic mentors were James Cone and James Sanders. There is little doubt that my sermon content reflects their influence. For the first ten years of my ministry I was shaped by their views and values. For the last thirty years of my ministry I have planned, prepared, and preached my sermons under that same influence, sometimes with the sense that they were looking over my shoulder to be sure I was still drawing from their wisdom and experience.

I fully understand that preaching on matters of social justice comes less easily and burns less urgently for preachers who may never have had mentors who pointed them in that direction. It is for that reason that they should look to the biblical example of bold speech captured in the example of Moses. The primary reason why Moses is remembered and celebrated is because of his bold speech, his *parrhesia* when he stood before Pharaoh demanding freedom for God's people. Even if a preacher never had a mentor who lifted the themes of justice, human rights, and liberation from all forms of oppression, the content of the Scriptures alone should lead that preacher to this conclusion.

From Moses standing before Pharaoh, to Deborah standing before Barak, to Samuel before Saul, Nathan before David, Jeremiah before Zedekiah, John the Baptist before Herod Antipas, and Paul before Festus and Agrippa, there is a one-thousand-year legacy of preachers who were willing to speak truth to power. They were willing to stand with "the least of these" and be a voice for the voiceless in society. This has been especially true for the American pulpit, where preachers have spoken out time and time again on matters of national importance: slavery, women's suffrage, child labor abuses, the care for the poor and destitute, and the wastefulness of war and endless military spending.

Liberty and Justice for All!

In an editorial entitled "Rekindling the American Conscience," Michael Gerson reminds us about the core values of this nation, values that are not in any way at odds with our values as Christians. He notes that Abraham Lincoln took particular interest in the phrase of the Declaration of Independence that says "life, liberty, and the pursuit of happiness." In doing so, said Lincoln, "They meant to set up a maxim for a free society, which should be familiar to all, and revered by all; constantly looked to, constantly labored for, even though never perfectly attained." Gerson wonders why this maxim was so important to Lincoln. He finds the answer in Lincoln's own words: "If liberty can be denied to anyone, it could eventually be denied to you!"[21] This phrase from Abraham Lincoln foreshadows the language of Martin Luther King Jr., who so frequently stated, "Injustice anywhere is a threat to justice everywhere."[22]

Michael Gerson finally states that "when our founding ideals are forgotten, it is the vulnerable and powerless who suffer first and worst."[23] He continues, "The greatness of America is a greatness of spirit. And its failures—such as slavery, segregation and the shameful treatment of Native Americans—are not only legal but spiritual failures. They are blasphemy against our country's creed."[24]

How much greater is the failure and how much worse is the blasphemy when we who are called to preach and to bear witness to the God of justice and liberation fail to speak on behalf of God and God's people.

Liberty Was Denied to Many in 1787

We must remember that on three of the four issues being raised in this section, even our nation's founders left the United States as an unfinished project. It would undoubtedly have been all four of the issues discussed in this chapter, except that the issues of LGBT had not yet emerged as part of the national conversation.

The language of the US Constitution is a reminder that from the beginning of this nation, when it came to the issues associated with Seneca Falls, Selma, and Standing Rock, liberty was denied explicitly to many people. Slavery and second-class citizenship for black Americans was written into the Constitution. In Article I, section 2, paragraph iii of that document, persons of African ancestry living in slavery were counted as three-fifths of a person for purposes of determining taxation and political representation for free white people. That same section clearly states, "Indians are excluded." Article I, section 9, paragraph I allowed the trans-Atlantic slave trade to continue until 1808, and Article IV, section 2, paragraph iii required that runaway slaves be returned to their owners.

While the Thirteenth Amendment to the Constitution abolished slavery, the Fourteenth Amendment limited the right to vote only to "male citizens" and continued to explicitly deny citizenship rights to Indians. When the Fifteenth Amendment extended voting rights to what was called "black suffrage," it included only black males. The right of women to vote was not established until the Nineteenth Amendment was ratified in 1920. The full citizenship rights of Native Americans, including the right to vote, did not come until the passage of the 1965 Voting Rights Act.[25]

Walk Together Children, Don't You Get Tired

When I was active in the civil rights movement of the 1960s, there were several songs that were relied upon to get people motivated and encouraged. The most famous of those songs was "We Shall Overcome." That song spoke of our hope that victory over racism and all its ugly manifestations would eventually be achieved. A second song proclaimed, "Like a tree planted by the water, I shall not be moved." That song was used to show our determination when opposing forces were telling us to go away and accept the status quo. Then there was this song:

> Walk together children, don't you get weary,
> There's a great camp meeting in the Promised Land.

There were other verses to that song accompanied by the same chorus: "Pray together children, walk together children, work together children, stay together children."[26] The purpose for that song was to encourage ourselves when we were becoming tired, disheartened, or secretly doubtful that change would come. The assurance was that if we persevered with our efforts even in the face of great difficulty and sometimes against overwhelming odds, we would be successful in achieving the just society that was our ultimate objective. It is reminiscent of Paul in Galatians 6:9 when he said, "Let us not become weary in doing good, for at the proper time we will reap a harvest if we do not give up."

Alan Aubrey Boesak of South Africa wrote the foreword to a book on prophetic preaching by Wendell Griffen, who is both a pastor and a circuit court judge in Arkansas.[27] In that foreword, Boesak writes both about the content of preaching and about the courage it takes to engage in the kind of preaching found in Griffen's book, and the kind of preaching that is also being encouraged here. Boesak mentions a comment

about the content of most preaching from the theologian Paul
Lehmann, who said:

> Most sermons are notably irrelevant. Sermons—even care-
> fully crafted ones—are nearly always event-less. They are
> a compound of either the obvious and the trivial, or the
> learned and the commonplace—or both—on the move from
> the latitudinous to the platitudinous. Everybody likes to
> hear what everybody knows—and effectively dismisses as
> not worth bothering about.[28]

Preaching that delves into the themes discussed in this chapter may at times be controversial, but they will seldom if ever
be irrelevant.

The question is whether preachers are willing to engage
in this kind of preaching, or will some preachers be content
with the "latitudinous and the platitudinous"? That is where
Boesak's second point comes into play. Speaking about the
content of Griffen's book and recalling the title of my book
Where Have All the Prophets Gone? Boesak said:

> The prophets have not all gone. Some of us may have got-
> ten lost; we may have been cowed by the power of empire
> or lured by the temptations of empire. Some of us may not
> have been able, unlike the midwives of Exodus 1, to over-
> come our fear of the empire with our love for the Lord, our
> trust of the Lord, and our commitment to following Jesus.
> But not all of us have gone.[29]

I urge every preacher to incorporate this kind of content
into their sermons and join the ranks of the prophets who
remain active and vocal in the twenty-first century. Evil will
not run away just because people seeking justice have shown
up. The devil will not surrender just because the saints join
the struggle. But if we can keep working, and preaching, and
praying, then the calls for justice that can be traced back
to the preaching of Moses will eventually bear good fruit.

Finding the courage to engage in this kind of preaching is all part of the making of a preacher.

▪ ▪ ▪

Notes

1. Doug Stanglin, "Harvard Social Club Revokes Membership for 9 Women, Reverts to All-Male Status," *USA Today*, July 7, 2017, https://www.usatoday.com/story/news/2017/07/07/harvard-fox-club-expels-9-women-reverts-all-male-status/458306001/.

2. Paul Raushenbush, "Christians, It's Time to Embrace the LGBTQ," *USA Today*, July 7, 2017, https://www.usatoday.com/story/opinion/2017/07/04/readers-best-comments-christians-its-time-embrace-lgbtq/450065001/.

3. Sheryl Gay Stolberg, "The Faces of Intermarriage, 50 Years After *Loving v. Virginia*," *The New York Times*, July 6, 2017, 10, https://www.nytimes.com/2017/07/06/us/the-faces-of-intermarriage-50-years-after-loving-v-virginia.html?mtrref=www.google.com&gwh=AE7832A2B5 6617DB212863D60BB1D023&gwt=pay.

4. Sheryl Gay Stolberg and Caitlin Dickerson, "Hangman's Noose, Symbol of Racial Animus, Keeps Cropping Up," *The New York Times*, July 5, 2017, 10, https://www.nytimes.com/2017/07/05/us/nooses-hate-crimes-philadelphia-mint.html.

5. David Weigel, "Trump's 'LGBT Rights' Promises Were Tied to the War on 'Radical Islam,'" *The Washington Post*, July 26, 2016, https://www.washingtonpost.com/.

6. Adam D. Chandler, "Donald Trump Just Sent a Painful Message to Me and Other LGBT People," *USA Today*, July 7, 2017, https://www.usatoday.com/story/opinion/2017/07/03/president-trumps-pride-month-adam-chandler-column/442577001/.

7. Daniel Burke, "Can This Priest Persuade Church Leaders to Welcome Gay Catholics?" CNN, July 6, 2017, https://www.cnn.com/2017/07/06/living/martin-gay-catholics/index.html.

8. Ibid.

9. Sharon Otterman, "Cardinals on Opposite Sides of the Hudson Reflect Two Paths of Catholicism," *The New York Times*, July 16, 2017, https://www.nytimes.com/2017/07/16/nyregion/cardinals-catholicism-same-sex-attraction-gay.html.

10. Marvin A. McMickle, "With Liberty and Justice for All," *The Christian Citizen*, July/August 2017, https://medium.com/christian-citizen/with-liberty-and-justice-for-all-cdafaa364ac6.

11. Robinson Meyer, "The Standing Rock Sioux Claim 'Victory and Vindication' in Court," *The Atlantic*, June 14, 2017, https://www.theatlantic.com/science/archive/2017/06/dakota-access-standing-rock-sioux-victory-court/530427/.

12. Donald A. Grinde Jr., "The Indian Removal Act," in *The Oxford Companion to United States History*, ed. Paul S. Boyer (New York: Oxford University Press, 2001), 378–79.

13. Julian Brave NoiseCat, "13 Issues Facing Native People Beyond Mascots and Casinos," HuffPost.com, August 31, 2015, https://www.huffingtonpost.com/entry/13-native-american-issues_us_55b7d801e4b0074ba5a6869c.

14. Eli Rosenberg, "Andrew Jackson Was Called 'Indian Killer.' Trump Honored Navajos in Front of His Portrait," *Chicago Tribune*, November 28, 2017, 1.

15. Felicia Fonseca and Laurie Kellman, "Families of Navajo Code Talkers Stunned by Trump's 'Pocahontas' Jab," *The Denver Post*, November 28, 2017, https://www.denverpost.com/2017/11/28/donald-trump-pocahontas-elizabeth-warren/.

16. Ibid.

17. *Windtalkers*, Metro Goldwyn Mayer, 2002.

18. *Flags of Our Fathers*, DreamWorks Pictures, 2006.

19. Ian MacDougall, "Should Indian Reservations Give Local Cops Authority on Their Land?" *The Atlantic*, July 19, 2017, https://www.theatlantic.com/politics/archive/2017/07/police-pine-ridge-indian-reservation/534072/.

20. Ibid.

21. Michael Gerson, "Rekindling the American Conscience," *The Democrat and Chronicle*, July 7, 2017, 9A.

22. Martin Luther King Jr., "Letter from Birmingham Jail," in *Why We Can't Wait* (New York: Signet Books, 1964), 77.

23. Abraham Lincoln, quoted in Michael Gerson, "Rekindling the American Conscience," *The Democrat and Chronicle*, July 7, 2017.

24. Ibid.

25. Marvin A. McMickle, "Who Are the People?" *Democrat and Chronicle*, July 30, 2017, 33A.

26. Evelyn Simpson-Currenton, arranger, "Walk Together Children," in *African American Heritage Hymnal* (Chicago: GIA Publications, 2001), 541.

27. Wendell Griffen, *The Fierce Urgency of Prophetic Hope* (Valley Forge, PA: Judson Press, 2017).

28. Alan Aubrey Boesak, "Foreword," ix.

29. Ibid., xi.

Chapter 7

Preaching Is Always Done in a Context

The LORD said to Moses, "When you return to Egypt, see that you perform before Pharaoh all the wonders I have given you the power to do. But I will harden his heart so that he will not let the people go." —Exodus 4:21, NIV

■ ■ ■

There is a direct link between the content of our sermons and the contexts in which those sermons are delivered. Preaching does not occur in a sociopolitical void where the circumstances that surround both the pulpit and the pew are irrelevant. Quite to the contrary, there must always be a clear understanding of the ways in which the content of our sermons has immediacy and relevance to the contexts in which people live every day. To quote Paul Tillich again, "Preaching must always be done with an awareness of the present moment."[1] That present moment involves the political, economic, cultural, and even theological questions that are swirling throughout the community and the country. Karl Barth asks, "What demands does the contemporary situation make on the preacher and his [or her] congregation? Together they are sharing a historical experience; the words of the preacher must be relevant to immediate preoccupations of his [or her] hearers."[2]

What is being argued here is that the context for preaching is not limited to the single question of the physical location in which the preacher is situated when the sermon is being delivered; though that issue will be discussed at some length in this chapter. Rather, the context has to do with everything that affects the values and views of the people to whom we preach both before they enter the sanctuary on a Sunday morning and after they leave the church and are immediately reimmersed into a society that is both highly secular on the one hand but also multifaith on the other.

Moses Preached within a Specific Context

As we continue to focus on Moses as the model for how preachers should function today, we need to pay close attention not only to the content of his message but also to the cultural and political contexts in which that message was delivered. Moses was demanding freedom for an enslaved people at the seat of power of the very nation that was benefitting from that slave labor. More importantly, Moses was not preaching about freedom for the Hebrews slaves from the safe confines of Mount Horeb (Sinai), which was hundreds of miles away. Nor was he preaching in the places where the slave population resided and where no one in authority in the Egyptian government was likely to hear his words. Instead, Moses took his message of liberation directly to the palace of Pharaoh, the most powerful man in the most powerful nation in the world at that time. Moses was standing amid the pomp and pageantry that surrounded an absolute monarch.

The Political Context

In thinking about the pharaoh of Egypt in the twelfth century BCE, it is important that twenty-first-century CE readers not think about democratic societies with co-equal branches of government. We should not think about the remaining monarchs of Europe whose power has long since been transferred to an elected parliament or some other national assembly. As much as presidents and prime ministers might want to rule their countries with absolute authority, the fact is becoming clearer with every passing day that they cannot demand that other elected officials vote in a certain way or have them removed from office if they do not conform to the demands and expectations of the head of state. Germany during the years of Adolf Hitler and the Third Reich, Russia during the days of Joseph Stalin, or North Korea under Kim Jung Un and his father and grandfather before him more accurately reflect the context into which Moses was sent. It is this encounter between Moses and Pharaoh that typifies the often-used phrase "speaking truth to power." The only power and authority recognized by most people assembled in that setting belonged to Pharaoh.

The Religious Context

In addition to the political power of Pharaoh, there was the polytheistic religion of ancient Egypt marked by a belief in and service to many different gods. There was no sense in Egypt of obedience to a single deity. There were many gods in their cosmology and theology that had to be placated and pacified. Taken together, this made ancient Egypt an unfriendly and unwelcoming setting for the message about freedom being demanded by a God understood in terms of monotheism that Moses had come to proclaim. And yet, in that context with the assurance of the presence of God and with the assistance of his brother Aaron, Moses delivered his message of liberation.

This unfriendly context was on display from the start. When Moses said to Pharaoh, "This is what the LORD, the God of Israel, says: 'Let my people go'" (Exodus 5:1, NIV), it is interesting to note that Pharaoh's first response was not anger at Moses and Aaron for what they had said to him. Pharaoh did not seem to take Moses seriously enough to express any anger over the lack of deference that had been paid to him. Instead, his first response was to refuse the demand made by Moses and to express contempt for the God who had sent Moses and Aaron to the palace. Pharaoh helps us understand the context in which Moses was preaching when he says, "Who is the LORD, that I should heed him and let Israel go? I do not know the LORD and I will not let Israel go" (Exodus 5:2, NIV). Moses was not addressing someone who was familiar with the legacy of Abraham, Isaac, and Jacob. Moses was not in a setting where the power and popularity of

Joseph was remembered or revered. The chilling line in Exodus 1:8 (NIV) makes that clear: "Then a new king, to whom Joseph meant nothing, came to power." Moses was preaching in a hostile context.

Just as important was the fact that Moses was preaching in a context that was dominated by an entirely different set of religious values. When Moses threw his staff on the ground before Pharaoh and the staff became a snake, Pharaoh's sorcerers and magicians, relying on their faith in the power of other gods, performed the same act (Exodus 7:11-12). There were dozens of gods honored by the people of Egypt. Among them were Isis, Osiris, Ra, Amun, Seth, and Karnak.[3] There was no familiarity in Egypt with the God who had sent Moses, and there was no sense of what we would call monotheism or the belief in the existence of just one god. Thus, the content of the preaching of Moses was spoken into a context in which his words were met with scorn on the one hand and with competing religious voices and values on the other. That was his context.

The Community Context

It must not be overlooked that Moses faced something else in his ministry context that would be just as problematic as the politics and polytheism of ancient Egypt. Moses also had to contend with the criticisms he faced coming from the very people he was trying to liberate from slavery. Those criticisms came in waves as the story of the exodus unfolds. The criticism began after Pharaoh told the Hebrew people to make bricks without straw, punishing them for what Moses had said about setting them free. They said, "May the LORD look upon you and judge you! You have made us obnoxious [a stench or bad odor, in other translations] to Pharaoh and his officials and have put a sword in their hands to kill us" (Exodus 5:21, NIV). It continued in Exodus 14:11-12 when the people perceived themselves to be trapped between the advancing Egyptian army and the waters of the Red Sea. They said, "Was it because there were no graves in Egypt that you brought us to the desert to die? . . . It would have been better for us to serve the Egyptians than to die in the desert" (NIV).

Not long after the miraculous crossing of the Red Sea, the complaining began again over a shortage of food and water: "In the desert the whole community grumbled against Moses and Aaron. . . . 'If only we had died by the LORD's hand in Egypt! There we sat around pots of meat and ate all the food we wanted, but you have brought us out into this desert to starve this entire assembly to death'" (Exodus 16:2-3, NIV).

One chapter later, in Exodus 17:2-3 (NIV), the complaining resumed: "But the people were thirsty for water there, and they grumbled against Moses. They said, 'Why did you bring us out of Egypt to make us and our children and livestock die of thirst?'" At this point, Moses grumbled at God and says, "What am I to do with these people? They are almost ready to stone me" (v. 4, NIV).

Preachers should take note of this pattern. Part of the making of a preacher is realizing that not every sermon that is preached, or every program that is planned, or every personnel move that is suggested will be welcomed with open arms. People in the church will grumble and complain about almost anything. They will complain about the music, about the length of the sermon, about the temperature in the sanctuary, about any change in the order of worship or the administration of the church. They will complain about the behavior or appearance of the pastor's spouse or children. They will complain about having too many or too few business meetings. They will complain about sermons that have either too much or too little social or political content. If there is one thing I learned during my thirty-four years as pastor of two local churches, it is that church people will complain over matters that are of major and minor importance.

Not all of the resistance that Moses faced came from outside the Hebrew community. It did not all come from Pharaoh and priests of polytheism. Much of it came from the very people on whose behalf he was working. Get ready. The same thing will happen to every preacher sooner or later!

The Times, They Are A'changing

There is another contextual issue that preachers today need to consider, and that is the rapid change in the religious landscape in the United States. In his 2016 article in *The Atlantic* titled "The Eclipse of White Christian America," Robert P. Jones talks about the declining influence of the Christian church and the Christian preacher. He begins by stating: "For most of the country's history, white Christian America—the cultural and political edifice built primarily by white Protestant Christians—set the tone for our national conversations and shaped American ideals." He then goes on to ask an important question: "The key question is why white Protestantism as a whole—arguably the most powerful cultural force in the history of the United States—has faded?"[4]

Jones points to three factors to account for this reality. The first is a declining interest in religion of any kind among young white Americans.[5] The second is what he calls the changing face of American religion marked by the rise in the percentage of black and Hispanic members of various Protestant denominations and independent churches.[6] Third, he notes that mainline and evangelical Protestants are getting older. When taken together, the numerical decline of white Protestants, matched by the loss of interest in religion by young people of all racial groups, greatly overshadows the continuing strength of African American and Hispanic Protestant groups.[7] This reality of the declining influence of and interest in religion in American society must be considered by those who would seek to preach the gospel of Jesus Christ.

I should note that while the influence of religion is declining in the measurable areas of church attendance, financial support, and adherence to certain doctrinal principles and practices, there is one area and one sector of American society where the influence of religion may be increasing. There is a growing influence of white evangelical Christians on the American political process. Both as a voting bloc and as a cultural force, this group of Christians has been growing in influence as they push back against broadening societal support for women's reproductive rights, LGBT rights, and the increasing multicultural and multifaith nature of US society.

Hints of this use of religion to oppose issues ranging from evolution to the proper role and curriculum of public schools can be traced back to the 1925 Scopes trial in Dayton, Tennessee, where a public-school teacher was charged, tried, and convicted because he taught his students about Charles Darwin and the theory of evolution.[8] However, the so-called Religious Right began to function as a political force in the 1980s with the emergence of the Moral Majority under Jerry Falwell. More will be said about the influence of "politicized evangelicalism" in the next chapter.[9] There is a fascinating discussion of the rise of white evangelicals as a political force in *Fantasyland* by Kurt Anderson.[10]

Mary Sanchez in a syndicated column points out how instrumental white evangelical Christians were in the 2016 presidential election. She states, "In 2016, evangelicals played a key role in delivering the nation Donald Trump as president. More than 80 percent of white evangelicals cast their ballots supporting Trump according to exit polling."[11] Sanchez continues by noting that a group called the American Renewal Project are actively recruiting conservative preachers "to stretch beyond the pulpit and campaign for GOP seats" at all levels of government. This is being encouraged in order to "restore a Judeo-Christian culture to the country."[12]

She also pointed out the difficulty of persons who claim a level of holiness or godliness supporting a man who is "an admitted groper of women, along with other patent indications of personal corruption."[13] She continues by noting, "It is difficult for many Americans to understand how evangelicals can possibly believe that Trump is standing up for Christian morality and principles."[14] Her final observation may be the most damning so far as white evangelical support of Trump is concerned. Rather than caring about Christian values, "it appears that he has used them just as he has used and abused so many suckers before in his reckless career."[15]

Preaching in a Postmodern World

Our twenty-first-century preaching context in the United
States is defined by a steady weakening of religious influence
on everything from the content of movies and television and
popular music, to the steady decline of church attendance
and of financial support for religious institutions. Graham
Johnston states that preaching in the twenty-first century is
done at a time when "two-thirds of Americans no longer
believe in objective truth."[16] How strange that the decline in
the acceptance of objective truth and the outcomes of science
is matched by the introduction of the term "fake news." This
is the term that allows people in power to discredit and thus
dismiss any criticism leveled against them by the news media.

Atheism is growing at about the same rate that persons
are leaving organized religious communities.[17] It has also
been observed that more theological conversation occurs in a
coffee shop after a movie than around the dinner table after
a Sunday sermon.

> Conversation about God—what we have traditionally called
> theology—is increasingly found outside the church as well
> as within it. One of the chief venues for such conversation is
> the movie theatre with its adjacent cafes. With attendance
> at church stagnating and with movie viewing at theatres
> and through video stores at an all-time high, Christians
> find themselves wanting to get back into the conversation
> but often are unable to do so effectively.[18]

The discussion about the ways in which culture influences
and even supplants the message of Christ did not begin in
recent years. As far back as 1966, H. Richard Niebuhr was
wrestling with this problem in *Christ and Culture*. He offered
five ways by which this issue could be approached: (1) Christ
against culture, which is how some fundamentalists might approach the problem. (2) Christ and culture in paradox, where
some middle ground is always being sought. (3) Christ the
transformer of culture, which suggests that God has ordained

certain worldly institutions, and the church must live with those institutions as best as it can, without sacrificing one's core values. (4) Christ above culture, where the sacraments of the church usher a person into a sacred space that culture cannot replicate. (5) The Christ of culture, which involves the cultural values and norms that serve as common ground between the church and society. The notion of a civil religion might well fit into this final category.[19]

Society Is Leaving the Church Behind

It may not be an overstatement to assert that over the five decades since Niebuhr's book first appeared, this nation may have shifted into a sixth category in terms of Christ and culture, and that would be a "Christ-less culture" in which many persons in society no longer give any consideration to what the church or the preacher has to say. This becomes apparent as society takes the lead in trending toward more openness and acceptance of things such as women's reproductive rights and same-sex marriage, things which many inside the church still openly and vocally oppose.

It is also quite likely that the church's continued resistance to the idea of women in ministry has resulted in more and more people viewing the church as a relic of the past in a society that has long since moved beyond such questions. Women now serve in the United States Senate, on the United States Supreme Court, as infantry officers in deployed units of the US Marine Corps and among Army Rangers, as president not only of Smith and Wellesley colleges but also of Harvard and Princeton. They serve as astronauts, police chiefs, national news anchors, and CEOs of major corporations like General Motors. It seems pointless to expect persons to enter a time warp on Sunday morning and go to a church where women are relegated to second-class status. This is a self-inflicted wound concerning which the church needs an immediate remedy of inclusion, equality, and leadership opportunities for all persons regardless of race or gender or sexual orientation.

The church and the preacher should not abandon attempts to reach this world with the gospel, but this context needs to be clearly understood if we expect to have any chance of being taken seriously. The apparent popularity of a handful of megachurch preachers should not lead anyone to doubt the challenges faced by most churches and most preachers in most places across this country.

The Church Faces Twenty-Four-Hour Competition

It should be noted that the context in which preaching is occurring in the twenty-first century is far more influenced by CNN and ESPN, by Netflix and Hulu, by podcasts and other forms of social media than it is by what is being preached from the pulpits of churches across the United States. Our sermons may last for fifteen to thirty minutes, and our Sunday worship services may run from one hour to more than three hours. That is no match for the access that church members and society at large have to social media, cable television news, and satellite talk radio that broadcast around the clock, twenty-four hours every day!

We should keep preaching, but we are doing so from a very different position than those of earlier generations who were preaching into a society that was much less hostile or indifferent to their message. Our posture seems to be what Jesus is saying in Revelation 3:20 (NIV), which proclaims, "Here I am! I stand at the door and knock. If anyone hears my voice and opens the door, I will come in and eat with that person, and they with me."

The Rise of the "Nones"

The declining influence of the church and the preacher is most visible by the rise of a new term in our cultural vocabulary: "nones." Consider the following facts: "The religiously unaffiliated, called 'nones,' are the second largest religious group in North America. In the United States, nones make up almost a quarter of the population. In the past decade, US nones have overtaken Catholics, mainline Protestants, and all followers of non-Christian faiths."[20]

At the same time, there has been a steady increase in the forms of spiritual practices made available to persons who may have begun their faith journey inside a Christian denomination. Some people have turned to the other two branches of the Abrahamic tradition, Islam and Judaism. Some have turned to Buddhist meditation or African religious rituals including Santeria and Vodun. Other people are being drawn to Wiccan practices. There is a steady growth of persons whose spiritual life is defined by humanism, which includes a community of believers but excludes the role of a deity. However, for an increasing number of persons who are asked to self-identify themselves in terms of religious affiliation, the answer is increasingly this one word: none!

Who Owns Sunday Morning?

There was at a time when the Christian church could be said to own Sunday morning. I use that phrase to demonstrate how dramatically things have changed. In the feature film *Concussion*, the fictional commissioner of the National Football League seeks to assert the importance and power of the NFL by saying, "We now own Sunday. That is the day that used to belong to God."[21] In a recent *Wall Street Journal* article about the problem of concussions among football players, the question was raised, could football ever end? Given that prospect, Jason Gay wondered, "Without football what the heck happens to Sunday?"[22]

The fact that fewer and fewer people see Sunday as the time to go to church does not mean that people are doing nothing on that day. There was a time in this country when Sunday morning was a protected time for those who wanted to attend worship services in a Christian church. There were so-called blue laws that restricted the secular activities that could occur at any time on Sunday.[23] This was done to allow either for a Sabbath rest or for church attendance free of any competing activities. Allowing for a certain hyperbole, it is undoubtedly true that the appeal of professional sports in the United States places great stress on the church both in terms of those who attend church with their eye on the clock, and those for whom a football game and the tailgate activities that precede the game may be their preferred activity on Sunday.

Preaching in an NFL City

I had the privilege of serving a Baptist congregation in a New Jersey suburb of New York City from 1976 to 1986, and another Baptist congregation in Cleveland, Ohio, from 1987 to 2011. I quickly learned what it means to be a pastor in a city with an NFL team (two in New York City where the New York Jets actually play in New Jersey) whose home game kickoffs are at 1 p.m. Some members told me that they would never be at church when the Cleveland Browns were playing a home game, because they had to be in their seats at the stadium or in front of their television sets before the ball was kicked off.

Indeed, the pressure was no less intense when the Jets, the Giants, or the Browns were playing out of town. People could not wait to get out of church so they could tune in to watch the game. On more than a few occasions, I saw members of the church tap their watches or point to the clock on the wall as a way of encouraging me to wrap up my sermon so they could get to the game. I confess that I never once conceded to their demands, which may be why some persons didn't show up at church on game day or why others streamed out of the sanctuary even before the benediction had been given.

The problem for churches in major metropolitan areas is that there are multiple professional sports franchises in those cities: the National Football League, National Basketball Association, Major League Baseball, National Hockey League, the Women's National Basketball Association, and various soccer and lacrosse leagues as well. This says nothing about the explosion of youth sports events such as soccer, lacrosse, hockey, softball, and track and field that now routinely schedule their events throughout the day on Sunday.

Thus, a year-round presence of sports programming competes with the Sunday morning worship service and any other events that might be planned for later Sunday afternoon or evening. I am not for a moment suggesting that we concede Sundays to the above-named activities, but I am saying that they are a formidable competitor for the time and attention of the people we would hope to draw into our churches. In such a context as this, it is even more important that our sermon content be as compelling and engaging as possible.

Sundays and the News Media

Professional sports are not the only cultural icons that seek to claim ownership of Sundays. At least two media outlets explicitly claim Sunday as belonging to them. There is a Sunday morning news program on NBC whose slogan is, "If it is Sunday it is 'Meet the Press.'" For a great many years now, a major national newspaper has used the slogan that says, "Sunday is for *The New York Times*." International news organizations have no hesitation in inviting people to spend their Sundays either watching a televised news program or digesting a massive Sunday edition of the newspaper. It would be fair to say that in our multi-faith society, not all people who engage in religious practices do so on Sunday. Muslims, Jews, Buddhists, and even the Seventh-Day Adventists and other "Sabbath-day" groups are not impacted by competing events on Sunday. However, for those who have historically viewed Sunday as their day of worship, their context is rapidly changing.

Here again, the issue is not to concede Sunday to the consumption of news or to be cowed by the competition news organizations present for the time and attention of the people we are trying to reach. The point is that we need to be crystal clear about the context in which we are attempting to preach the gospel. It may well be that our sermons might have greater effect if we were to incorporate into our sermons some references to, some illustrations from, some analogies between, and even some biographical stories about persons in the news or on one of the major sports teams. We need to bring a moral or a sharp prophetic critique to the events being reported in the news. We might be able to use a sport like football to draw attention to some issue in the church.

Sports Analogies Can Go a Long Way

I have often tried to encourage church members to appreciate that every task that needs to be done in the church is important, whether it comes with a lot of attention and recognition or not. I remind them of how many football games come down to the closing seconds and everything hinges on making a field goal. At that point, multimillion-dollar quarterbacks are of no further value. Massively muscled linemen must kneel on the sidelines and watch. The whole team is now depending on three people whose names are not popular but whose work is essential if the team is going to win the game: the long snapper, the holder, and the kicker.

The long snapper must get the ball perfectly positioned into the hands of the holder. The holder must catch the snap and get the ball into the right position for the kicker. The kicker must make the right approach to the ball and kick into a very narrow space that may be fifty yards down the field. Most fans and even sportswriters know very little about those three players, because we are so fixated on the superstar players with the big salaries. As I have traveled around the country where NFL teams are located, I have asked people to name the long snapper on their team. Most people have never heard of that position, much less know the name of which player fills that role. But it is amazing how many games have been won or lost beginning with the work of the unknown long snapper. Such an analogy transfers well into the life of the church where people are being urged to serve without worrying about their task being less important than the work being done by others. Every job in the church is important.

Consider the story in Acts 1:15ff where the replacement of Judas comes down to two potential candidates, Justus and Matthias. There is an important lesson that can be communicated in our sermons based upon the previous analogy involving football's lesser-known positions. Matthias was the person who was selected, even though Justus was equally qualified. People all over the world have heard the names of Peter, James and John. There are cities, schools, hospitals, churches, and children named after those well-known apostles of Jesus.

On the other hand, few if any people have any knowledge that anyone named Matthias was numbered among the apostles of Jesus. Nevertheless, Matthias was just as faithful as

Peter even though his name is rarely if ever mentioned. Matthias went into the world preaching the gospel. Matthias may well have faced the same hostilities, perhaps even the same martyrdom as Peter and the other better-known apostles. There are people in every church just as there are players on every football team who are like Matthias, serving faithfully with much less notoriety or public recognition. This notion of lesser-known players who contribute to winning the game applies just as easily to substitutes coming off the bench in a basketball game, or to a pinch hitter or pinch runner in a baseball game. Applying these kind of illustrations and analogies from the world of sporting events can help bridge the gap between those two competing worlds of church and society.

Learn from the Early Christian Church

This is the context in which we must learn to do our preaching. We must be able to speak the name of Jesus, not only in the midst of a culture that does not want to honor any religion at all but also in a culture where the virtues of other religious traditions and practices are being touted every day. In this regard, our task is similar to that of the early church and the first generation of apostles. The Christian faith was not born into a welcoming and inviting context where its message was received gladly by all who heard the gospel being preached. Instead, the name of Jesus was actively suppressed by many who wanted to prevent his message from being heard.

Acts 4 reports the travails of Peter and John, who were imprisoned in Jerusalem because they were preaching in the name of Jesus, and who were released only on the condition that they "speak no more to anyone in this name" (Acts 4:17). In Acts 5 Peter and those with him were arrested again. In Acts 7 Stephen was stoned for preaching about Jesus. In Acts 9 Saul was converted on the road to Damascus, but he had been headed there to arrest those who preached about Jesus. In Acts 12 Herod had James the brother of Jesus killed by the sword. It is believed that Paul, who had suffered much for the preaching of the gospel as recounted in 2 Corinthians 11:23-29, was finally beheaded in the city of Rome.

Not only was the world hostile to the message of the early church, but there was stiff competition for the hearts and minds of people from the other religions being practiced at that time. In Acts 17:22-23 Paul refers to the many gods whose names were known, as well the unknown god that was being worshipped by the people of Athens. He mentions the Epicureans, who were famous for their love of the pleasures of life, as well as the Stoics, who were equally famous for refraining from such things. In Acts 19 Paul created a riot in the city of Ephesus when he appeared to be drawing people away from Artemis, the local deity of that city.

So, whether the issue was intolerance toward the preaching of the gospel or the competing religious voices that were clamoring for the attention of people, the world of the early church was very much like the current context in which we are being called to preach. Learning how to preach and then daring to preach Christ boldly and confidently in this twenty-first-century context is part of what is involved in the making of a preacher. Such preaching is how the Christian faith was birthed and spread throughout the world. We should not be the least bit hesitant to follow the example of the first-century apostles as we seek to exalt the name and spread the message of Jesus in the twenty-first century. In this sense, Ecclesiastes 1:9 is true, "There is nothing new under the sun." Learning that lesson and becoming comfortable in preaching in multiple social, political, and even ecclesiastical contexts is part of the process in the making of a preacher.

Notes

1. Paul Tillich, quoted in Karl Barth, *The Preaching of the Gospel* (Philadelphia: Westminster Press, 1963), 54.
2. Karl Barth, 54.
3. "Ancient Egyptian Gods and Goddesses," Discovering Egypt, https://discoveringegypt.com/ancient-egyptian-gods-and-goddesses/.com; "Egypt," in *The Interpreter's Dictionary of the Bible*, vol. 2 (Nashville: Abingdon, 1962), 56–66.
4. Robert P. Jones, "The Eclipse of White Christian America," *The Atlantic*, July 21, 2016, https://www.theatlantic.com/politics/archive/2016/07/the-eclipse-of-white-christian-america/490724/.

5. Ibid.
6. Ibid.
7. Ibid.
8. Edward J. Larson, "Scopes Trial," *The Oxford Companion to United States History* (New York: Oxford University Press, 2001), 693.
9. The term comes from James A. Sanders, *The Re-birth of a Born-Again Christian* (Eugene, OR: Cascade Books, 2017), 115.
10. Kurt Anderson, *Fantasyland* (New York: Random House, 2017), 165–69, 198–208.
11. Mary Sanchez, "USA's Party of God Doubles Down on Trump," *Democrat and Chronicle*, December 22, 2017, 13A.
12. Ibid.
13. Ibid.
14. Ibid.
15. Ibid.
16. Graham Johnston, *Preaching to a Postmodern World* (Grand Rapids, MI: Baker Books, 2001), 9; cf. Robert Kysar and Joseph M. Webb, *Preaching to Postmoderns* (Peabody, MA: Hendrickson Publishers, 2006).
17. Gabe Bullard, "The World's Newest Major Religion: No Religion," *National Geographic*, April 22, 2016, https://news.nationalgeographic.com/2016/04/160422-atheism-agnostic-secular-nones-rising-religion/.
18. Robert K. Johnston, *Reel Spirituality: Theology and Film in Dialogue* (Grand Rapids, MI: Baker Books, 2000), 14.
19. John G. Stackhouse, "In the World, but . . . ," *Christianity Today*, April 22, 2002, citing https://news.nationalgeographic.com/2016/04/160422-atheism-agnostic-secular-nones-rising-religion/; H. Richard Niebuhr, *Christ and Culture* (New York: Harper and Row, 1951).
20. Ibid.
21. *Concussion*, Columbia Pictures, 2016.
22. Jason Gay, "Could Football Ever End?" *Wall Street Journal*, July 30, 2017, https://www.wsj.com/articles/could-football-ever-end-1501423731.
23. "Blue Law," *Encyclopedia Britannica*, https://www.britannica.com/topic/blue-law.

Chapter 8

Preaching in the Present Moment

> [Jesus] replied, "It is not for you to know the times or periods that the Father has set by his own authority. But you will receive power when the Holy Spirit has come upon you; and you will be my witnesses in Jerusalem, in all Judea and Samaria, and to the ends of the earth." When he had said this, as they were watching, he was lifted up, and a cloud took him out of their sight. —Acts 1:7-9

■ ■ ■

In discussing context, I am urging preachers to consider both their willingness and then their ability to preach in multiple settings and before multiple audiences. Preachers are made as they develop the willingness to preach to teens around a campfire at a summer camp, as they are preaching to skeptics and seekers in a college chapel, as they are bringing a brief message to residents in a senior citizen center. Preachers are made when they are willing to preach in places outside of their own denomination, their own racial group, and even their own preferred theological context. Preachers should accept the invitation to speak at interfaith gatherings and boldly represent the values of the Christian faith, knowing for certain that representatives of other faith traditions will be doing the same.

Physical Location Is Part of Our Context

Let's begin with the easiest part of this discussion: context most certainly begins with the physical locations in which our preaching takes place. The true measure of a great preacher is not how well that person preaches on a Sunday morning in their own local church and before the familiar faces of their own congregation. Preachers need to learn from the example of Jesus, John the Baptist, Paul, Peter and John, and the other leaders of the early church. They did not remain confined inside of house churches where they were essentially preaching to the converted. Those New Testament preachers stood on street corners, on mountainsides, along the shores of rivers and streams. They preached both inside and outside of palaces and government buildings. If the gospel is to have any major impact on today's world, it will have to be spoken and preached beyond the confines of a pulpit inside a sanctuary on Sunday morning.

Preachers are made when they are as willing to bring a word of encouragement to prisoners inside a correctional facility as they are to bring a word of renewal to a group of believers gathered outdoors in a tent for a revival meeting. Preaching for some may involve sitting in a radio broadcast booth by yourself while you imagine the people who are listening to the message you are delivering through that medium as you speak into a microphone. Preaching for others may involve preaching in English while your words are being translated into another language by someone who is standing beside you.

Preaching to a Chinese-Language Congregation

I remember being invited to preach at The Chinese Christian Church of Cleveland, Ohio. I do *not* remember being told that very few members of that congregation were fluent in English and therefore a translator would be needed. He and I stood side by side during the sermon. I would say something in English and he would immediately translate my words into Mandarin. However, not all members of that church spoke Mandarin. Half of the congregation spoke Cantonese. Therefore, there was a person sitting in a booth in the back of the sanctuary wearing a set of headphones who would take the Mandarin translation of my sermon and translate it into

Cantonese, which was heard by Cantonese-speaking members of that congregation who were also wearing headsets. Members of my congregation had joined me for the service at the Chinese Christian Church of Cleveland, and all of us walked away with a new appreciation for the multicultural, multi-ethnic, and multilingual challenges of preaching.

I Wish I Had Studied Spanish

After all the years I spent studying French and German as a student, I now wish I had devoted myself to Spanish. Possessing fluency in that language could greatly expand a preacher's ability to present the gospel in this country with its rapidly increasingly Spanish-speaking population. Many longstanding black congregations located in urban areas are finding themselves challenged by the influx into those neighborhoods of Spanish-speaking groups from Mexico, the Dominican Republic, Puerto Rico, and countries throughout Central and South America. Those churches either must bring on a Spanish-speaking staffperson, move out of that rapidly changing neighborhood, or watch while a population grows around them that cannot be reached because of language differences. Persons who are considering careers in Christian ministry might well give some thought to learning a second language that can make them more impactful if they end up in a context where there is a non-English-speaking population; this could be Spanish or Arabic or Chinese.

In a Context of Gentrification

One of the pressures affecting preachers and churches in certain contexts is a rise in what is known as gentrification. This is a process where an urban, even an inner-city neighborhood is experiencing an influx of new residents of a higher income bracket and usually of a different racial group than the current neighborhood population. What tends to happen is that those urban properties can be purchased at a lower price because of their current condition due to a lack of investment in upgrades and improvements. New owners begin to improve those properties. The value of surrounding properties begins to increase. Eventually, because of increases in property taxes or in rent, current residents are no longer able to afford to live in those neighborhoods. New homeowners begin to attract new businesses that cater to their higher income status. Soon, what might have been an impoverished area has become an upscale community in which a steady population shift occurs.

As a *USA Today* article pointed out in 2017, gentrification has a direct effect on the churches in those areas.[1] A ninety-year-old African American congregation in Nashville typifies the problem. The church stands across the street from a new luxury apartment building. According to the pastor of that church:

> **The church's predominately black congregation once mirrored the neighborhood's demographics, but today the hip and eclectic East Nashville neighborhood, with its rising property values and trendy restaurants, draws a number of white millennials. . . . Many churches in this community are leaving. They are selling their churches to land developers who are turning them into restaurants and bars and condos and apartments and any number of things.[2]**

The church has tried to reach out and attract the new residents into their church, but cultural differences in terms of worship style often pose a problem. The church had a door-knocking campaign in the new apartment complex to invite residents to the church. According to the pastor, Morris Tipton Jr., "So far, only about five white people have accepted that invitation. They come and they generally don't come back because, again, more times than not, this is not the flavor of worship they've grown up with."[3] Often, a gentrified neighborhood will be accompanied by a new church startup by an existing suburban congregation that wants to reach those new urban residents. As a result, the existing church does not attract the new residents, and the new church is not especially interested in attracting the existing residents.

Preachers are made when they come to grips with this changing neighborhood landscape. They can decide to commit themselves to building a multiracial and economically diverse congregation. They can seek to maintain their present congregation even as members are forced to relocate out of the neighborhood. Several churches in the community can merge their memberships and operate out of only one building. They can sell their property and build a new facility in a different community that seems to offer demographic possibilities. Either way, the reality of gentrification is not going away.

In the Footsteps of Adoniram and Ann Judson

As an American Baptist, I am keenly aware of the missionary work of Adoniram and Ann Judson, who sailed for India in 1812 but moved inland to Burma to begin their work in 1813. Over a thirty-seven-year ministry, Adoniram translated the Bible into Burmese and began work on a Burmese dictionary, which he completed in 1849. He, Ann, his beloved first wife, and Sarah, his second wife, were largely responsible for introducing the gospel to Burma.[4] Today, there are large numbers of Burmese Christians who have fled the political upheavals in their home country (now known as Myanmar) and have settled in the United States.

Here in Rochester, New York, where I reside, the Lake Avenue Baptist Church has become home to a large Burmese membership who trace their lineage as Christians directly to the Judsons. Another large group has concentrated in nearby Utica, New York. This Burmese community breaks out into three language groups. When I was there to preach on a Sunday morning, all three language groups were given equal time in the worship service for songs, prayers, and responsive readings. This is not missionary work like the Judsons were engaged in where preachers sail to the other side of the world. This is preachers and congregations learning how to do ministry in their own local context which may very well find them trying to interact with believers who speak a language other than English.

This is undoubtedly the reason why Paul was sent out to be the apostle to the Gentiles. Paul was likely fluent in Greek as well as Hebrew and Aramaic. He could deliver the gospel to a broader audience than most of the other apostles, because he could address them in a language they understood. It is a tremendous benefit when a preacher can be fluent in more than one language. It is essential if the context of his or her local church includes non-English-speaking persons.

Our Context Includes Cultural Components

The context of our preaching is not just the physical locations in which we stand when we deliver our sermons. Our context is also the character and composition of the community in which our churches are located and in which our preaching is occurring. The context of an inner-city or urban congregation is not the same as ministry that is done in rural and agricultural settings. One of the lessons learned by the Democratic Party in the 2016 presidential election was the danger of believing that what people believe or value in New York City or Chicago or Los Angeles is the same as what people think or value in the little towns and farming communities scattered across the country. You cannot fly over everything between New York and Los Angeles and expect to win a national election. Different places face different pressures and problems, and knowing those contexts is as important for a preacher as it is for an aspiring presidential candidate.

Between 1972 and 1976 I was on the ministry staff of Abyssinian Baptist Church of New York City. Once the black Mecca of the United States, the Harlem community in which that church is located had fallen onto hard times with row upon row of dilapidated housing, shuttered businesses, an endless supply of liquor stores, and the continuing spread of heroin and the crack cocaine epidemic that soon followed. New York City itself was near a state of bankruptcy, and despair hung in the air like a cloud. There was no shortage of churches in Harlem, but there was a shortage of hope that things would get better.

Every time one of the ministers of that church got up to preach we knew one thing perfectly well: there would be someone in that congregation who had stopped by to give

Jesus one last hearing before they went from 138th Street, where we were, to 116th Street, where Louis Farrakhan was waiting for them. Muhammad's Temple #7 was a formidable competitor for the message of Jesus among young men and women in Harlem. That was the Temple where Malcolm X had served until 1964, and now it was home to Louis Farrakhan, the fiery and charismatic preacher in the Nation of Islam. That was our context. We never worried about losing one of our young people to another Protestant denomination, but in those days, we were concerned about losing them either to the Nation of Islam or to orthodox Islam instead.

Our sermons had to address the real-world challenges of the people who lived and worked in Harlem every day. We had to talk about police-community relations forty years before there was a Black Lives Matter movement. We had to address the fact that no major grocery store was in the community, and the meat and produce in the corner stores were certainly not fresh but were definitely overpriced. We had to preach funerals following gang-related violence, drug overdoses, suicides, a high rate of infant mortality, and people who died because of strokes and heart attacks rooted in bad diets and the stress of inner-city life.

A Black Man in Baraboo, Wisconsin

Most of my life has been spent in urban areas: in Chicago; in New York City; in a suburb just five miles from Newark, New Jersey; in Cleveland, Ohio; and now in Rochester, New York. However, I got an early introduction to valuing different cultural contexts when I was a student at Aurora College. I selected that school located sixty miles from Chicago because it gave me quick access back to my hometown, where I returned as often as I could. However, a requirement for graduating from that school as a ministry candidate was spending a summer immersed in a context that was different from the one you were most comfortable with.

Realizing my preference for the big city and the urban scene, my academic advisor arranged for me to be sent to an Advent Christian church in Baraboo, Wisconsin, the heart of America's dairy country. In the summer of 1969 I made the move from the Southside of Chicago, where the streets were crowded at all hours of the day and night and where the blues music blasted from the bars on both sides of the major avenues.

I arrived in a town of fewer than five thousand residents, and most of them lived outside of town on their farms. It was a culture shock indeed to be in a place where people went to bed at 8 p.m., woke up at 4:30 a.m., and preferred stock car racing and showcasing their animals at the county fair over Motown music and schoolyard basketball. I was the only African American living within that county. I was the first African American most people in Baraboo had ever seen live and in living color. For my first week in that tiny town, I was homesick, lonely, and woefully out of step with that pace of life. However, after a few trips to the milking barn at early morning hours to visit with church members, we began to know one another. I lived for one month with the pastor of the church, and the next month I lived with a family that provided hay for the dairy cows in the area. I saw milk being processed. I watched cheese being made. I witnessed the anxieties of people for whom summer rains were not an intrusion into a baseball game but were essential to their day-to-day survival as farmers.

I also learned that Baraboo was the winter home for the Ringling Brothers and Barnum & Bailey Circus. The stately homes of the Ringling brothers were still standing on the main street of the town. The Circus World Museum was their major visitors' attraction.

I, who had prided myself on my Brooks Brothers button-down-collar shirts and my khaki pants, was living in a world of overalls, caps that carried the name of heavy equipment companies, work boots, the constant smell of manure, and a worldview that had no connection whatsoever to the world I lived in back in Chicago. Their lives were tied to the Chicago Mercantile Exchange and the prices of the products they were making or the feed corn they had to buy. They were not getting in cars and driving to work in a downtown office building. They were revving up their tractors and their bailing machines and their milk processing plants.

My job was to be a part of the ministry team in that community. It was not helpful for me to preach to them about urban blight or failing inner-city schools. Their chief concerns were of their children leaving the farms and seeking opportunities elsewhere. They were concerned about alcoholism and depression and divorce and domestic violence. They were concerned about fields that were not as productive as in former years and about diseases that could spread through their animal herds. They were concerned about being able to pay for the farming equipment they were buying over time and whether one bad season could result in home foreclosures and repossession of their trucks and tractors and harvesters.

Fortunately, the Bible is full of material that can be called upon to prepare sermons and Bible studies in that context. Stories about barns, fields, farmers, crops and flocks, and living in harmony with nature can allow preachers to be effective in that context. I returned to Chicago before the summer of 1969 was over, but I returned a substantially different person. I had realized that not everyone lives in my context. Not everyone is worried about the things that trouble me. But whoever they are and wherever they live, they deserve a preacher who takes the time to learn about them and about their lives and about their particular place in the world.

So, whether your ministry is in New York City, or El Paso, Texas, or Cedar Rapids, Iowa, or Baraboo, Wisconsin, be faithful to and respectful of the people in that context. They need to hear the gospel addressed to them and their immediate context. They will likely listen when you seek to focus their attention elsewhere in the world if they know you are not ignoring or overlooking the place where they live every day.

Preaching in "Haunted Houses"

"Haunted houses" is a term coined by Walter Fluker as he describes the challenges facing African American churches in the twenty-first century. The secularization of society and its impact on church attendance and support may have first been felt by preachers and churches outside of the black community. However, according to Fluker, the same dynamics are being felt within African American communities today. "The memories of the past are no longer adequate to sustain the mission of black churches in these turbulent times."[5] His point is that the important role once played by black churches, especially during the civil rights movement, has not translated into continuing relevance in the era of the Black Lives Matter movement where leadership resides largely outside of the church and without seeking prior approval from the clergy. "The Black Lives Matter Movement was not initiated or led by church leaders, but mainly by young activists with moderate, if any, relationship with the church. In fact, Black Lives Matter was initiated by three black women, two of whom self-identify as queer."[6]

Fluker reinforces his point about the church as a haunted house by referring to the essay by Eddie Glaude Jr. of Princeton University entitled "The Black Church Is Dead."[7] Glaude argued, "Of course, many African Americans still go to church . . . But the idea of this venerable institution as central to black life as a repository for the social and moral conscience of the nation have all but disappeared."[8] Glaude supported his assertion, in part, by stating that "when memory becomes currency the result is all too often church services and liturgies that entertain, but lack a spirit that transforms, and preachers who deign for followers instead of fellow travelers in God."[9] In this context, Glaude still saw a ray of hope. He said:

> **The death of the black church as we have known it occasions an opportunity to breathe new life into what it means to be black and Christian. Black churches and preachers must find their prophetic voices in this momentous present. And in doing so, black churches will rise again and insist that we all assert ourselves on the national stage not as sycophants to a glorious past, but as witnesses to the ongoing revelation of God's love in the here and now as we work on behalf of those who suffer most.[10]**

Fluker suggests that achieving what Glaude has envisioned is the equivalent of "waking up the dead."[11] This is the current context in which so many African American preachers now find themselves: living on the memory of the way things were while failing to realize how much the world has changed around them.

When the National Museum of African American History and Culture opened in Washington, DC, in 2016, I was surprised to discover that a quote attributed to me appeared on one of the walls in the section dedicated to the role of the black church. The quote says, "Nineteenth-century black churches ministered to the needs of the soul and served a host of secular functions, which placed them squarely in the center of black social life."[12]

What Fluker and Glaude are saying, and what I must also concede in light of that quote on the wall of the museum, is that the black church no longer plays that same role as the center of the community. That is because the black church has repeatedly failed to address or adapt to the changes occurring in society, most notably the role of women and the whole issue of human sexuality. People will not come to church to be marginalized or condemned to hell. What they will do is spend their time and money elsewhere. It is unfortunate that there is a divide between the leaders of the Black Lives Matter movement and the pastoral leaders in most black communities. The truth is, twenty-first-century black activists are *not* going to be led by or lectured to by preachers who are stuck in a mid-twentieth-century worldview.

In truth, Fluker and Glaude were not the first ones to note that when the African American church moved away from its prophetic focus it would spell trouble for its future. More than fifty years ago, in 1964, Joseph Washington could already see this present scenario developing. In *Black Religion*, he stated:

> **For several generations now, Negro ministers and their congregations have misconstrued the historic intent of the folk religion. . . . Black religion has always been deeply**

committed to the central concern of Christianity . . . love – justice – equality . . . Black folk religion has dissipated into entertainment and the church has been relegated into an amusement center for disengaged Negroes.[13]

Part of that amusement and entertainment is an emerging preaching style where the objective is neither conversion of the soul nor commitment of the heart to the Christian life. Instead, it is preaching designed to elicit an emotional response from the congregation as an end in itself. I am not minimizing the historic use of zeal and emotion that has long been associated with preaching in many cultural settings. The idea of being caught up in the spirit while preaching is a powerful thing to behold or to experience. I commend readers of this book to the discussion about the place of celebration in preaching found in the writings of Frank Thomas, Henry Mitchell, and Cleophus LaRue.[14]

Often, however, those experiences come at the end of a sermon that has set forth a compelling and convicting message. When the only objective of a preacher for his or her sermon is to shout as loudly as possible, speak as rapidly as possible, bang the pulpit as frequently as possible, stomp their feet as often as possible, and generate as much vocal response as possible from the congregation, then the warnings from Eddie Glaude Jr., Walter Fluker, and Joseph Washington are being ignored, and their predicted outcomes are being realized; the decline in the influence of the church even in the African American community steadily continues.

Preaching in the Current Political Context

The election of Barack Obama was the most unexpected and overwhelming political event in my lifetime. Elsewhere I have observed that his election was one of the three most history-altering elections in American history.

The election of George Washington in 1789 was a definitive move away from monarchy. The election of Abraham Lincoln in 1860 set the nation on a course toward Civil War, the

> abolition of slavery and the preservation of the union. The
> election of Barack Obama, the nation's first African Ameri-
> can president, raised the specter that the United States was
> on its way to becoming a post-racial society. Was it possible
> that the blood and prayers and pleadings of freedom-loving
> people, black and white, that stretched from the abolition-
> ist movement of the 1830s through the Civil Rights Move-
> ment of the 1960s was finally bearing fruit?[15]

The answer to that question came with the election of Donald Trump, who has unleashed a revival of racial and regional
polarization that the election of Obama either masked or began to ignite. The only thing more surprising to me about the
election of the nation's first African American president was
that it was immediately followed by the election of the very
man who birthed "the birther movement" and did everything
in his power to discredit President Obama.

It was Donald Trump who said, "There were some very
fine people" among the Nazis and white nationalists who
marched in Charlottesville, Virginia, shouting the Nazi slogan
of "blood and soil."[16] It was Donald Trump who referred to
Haiti, all of Africa, and El Salvador as "shithole countries."[17]
It was Donald Trump who said that once people from Nige-
ria came to the United States, "they would never go back to
their huts in Africa."[18]

I agree with Wes Allen, who states that preachers must be
aware that the election of Donald Trump has "the potential
for significant harm to the ethical fabric of our society."[19] I
also agree with Allen when he points out that the election of
Donald Trump revealed not only that we are a divided nation
but also that "we are a divided church."[20]

Trump Voters Are in Every Church

The pews of many churches in the United States hold persons
who voted for Donald Trump. In fact, they may have voted
for him precisely because they agree with his views—views
that may be abhorrent to the preacher and to others in the
congregation. It is possible that white evangelical Christians

provided the margin of victory for Trump; a *Washington Post* poll reported that 80 percent of white persons who self-declare as evangelicals voted for Donald Trump.[21] Another sign of the divided church involved the number of black pastors who announced their support for Trump, even speaking on his behalf at the Republican National Convention in 2016.[22]

In other words, support for Trump comes not just from white nationalists such as Richard Spencer, who ended his pro-Trump speech in 2016 with a Nazi salute and the words "Hail Trump, Hail Our People, Hail Victory."[23] It is not just David Duke of the KKK who said, "Trump's victory is one of the most exciting nights of my life . . . Make no mistake about it, our people have played a HUGE role in electing Trump."[24] The election of Donald Trump was made possible by overwhelming support from people who sit in church every Sunday listening to sermons. This is part of the context in which preaching is occurring today. There is no Trump-free zone even within many of our churches.

The support of Trump by white, evangelical Christians was shamefully on display in the wake of the news that Donald Trump had authorized the payment of $130,000 to an adult film actress named Stormy Daniels. Two evangelical leaders, Franklin Graham and Tony Perkins defended Trump by saying "we will give him a mulligan", a golf term that means a second shot or a second chance. Perkins was offering corporate forgiveness to Trump even though Trump had neither acknowledged any misconduct or requested any forgiveness. Since when does the church offer the "assurance of pardon" to people who have never engaged in the "confession of sin?"[25] Yet, it can be claimed with certainty that "Donald Trump won the White House in 2016 , defying all predictions, in large part thanks to a groundswell of white evangelical turnout."[26] Estimates suggest that as much as 85% of the white evangelical vote went to a person whose lifestyle and life story are nearly 100% contrary to everything that conservative Christians have heretofore believed.[27]

One of the consequences of this development among white conservative Christians is the withdrawal of many African

Americans from white evangelical churches where support of Donald Trump was the decisive issue. Michael Emerson, co-author with Christian Smith of *Divided by Faith: Evangelical Religion and the Problem of Race in America*,[28] states, "The election itself was the single most harmful event to the whole movement of racial reconciliation in at least the past 30 years"[29] My former professor and mentor, James Sanders, makes a similar point about preaching to a divided church. He writes:

> The outcome of the national elections has revealed how great the divide is and will probably indicate how influential politicized evangelicalism has become over the last thirty years . . . I am greatly disturbed at how politicized to the radical right it has become—to its own detriment, to that of the country generally, and especially to the detriment of the American political process.[30]

Why Do White Evangelicals Support Trump?

When the 2016 presidential campaign began, Donald Trump was not the darling of white evangelical Christians. That role fell to Texas Senator Ted Cruz. As Michelle Goldberg wrote:

> This time a year ago, leaders of the old guard religious right were determined to stop Donald J. Trump from winning the Iowa caucuses. James Dobson of Focus on the Family and Tony Perkins of the Family Research Council campaigned with Ted Cruz. Prominent female anti-abortion activists released an open letter, "Pro-Life Women Sound the Alarm: Donald Trump Is Unacceptable."[31]

However, when Trump won the Republican Party nomination for president, these same persons became some of his most loyal backers. Goldberg surmises that religious conservatives "realized that their only path to federal influence lay in a bargain with this profane, thrice-married Manhattan sybarite. So, they got in line."[32] One of those leaders went so far as to say, "I believe Trump has been elected by divine intervention."[33]

However, Goldberg supports the claim of this chapter that organized religion in the United States is losing its influence. According to the Pew Research Center, barely a third of Republican voters who attended services weekly supported Mr. Trump. She continues:

> **He had consistent evangelical support, but it tended to come from less strongly affiliated Christians—people who might identify as born again, but who weren't connected to the congregations that once formed the building blocks of the religious right, and who didn't take marching orders from the movement's leaders.[34]**

Finally, she makes the case that "by winning the primary [Iowa] over the strenuous objections of prominent Christian conservatives, Mr. Trump revealed their diminishing sway."[35]

Mike Pence May Be Even Worse

Conservative Christians are not without a true champion in the current political context. Vice President Mike Pence is a card-carrying member of the religious right. While he had been raised as a Roman Catholic, he later embraced conservative Protestant evangelical views that included opposition to abortion in virtually all instances, support of Israel and non-support of the Palestinian state, the belief that the United States is a "Christian country," and support of the Religious Freedom Restoration Law. The latter allowed private businesses to turn away gay customers based upon religious objections to homosexuality. When he was governor of Indiana, Pence signed such a bill into law. However, after swift and strong opposition that once again reflected the diminishing influence of religion in American society, he was forced to revoke that bill and agree to a greatly modified version.[36]

Upon his election as vice president, Pence described himself as "a Christian, a conservative and a Republican, in that order, and as a born-again evangelical Catholic."[37] As proof of his conservative evangelical credentials, Pence handpicked Ralph Drollinger to lead a Bible study for members of Donald Trump's Cabinet. Drollinger is on record as saying that it is a sin for female lawmakers with young children at home to leave home to be involved in politics. He also declared that Roman Catholicism is one of the "primary false religions in the world."[38] And Drollinger's influence is not limited to Trump's Cabinet. Through the auspices of Drollinger's organization, known as Capitol Ministries, he has established these conservative Bible study groups in forty state capitols, and there is another group that meets in Washington, DC, that includes sixty-eight members of the US Senate and House of Representatives.[39] As much as some persons might disagree with the views or biblical interpretations of persons such as Ralph Drollinger, he represents part of that "politicized evangelicalism" discussed by James Sanders who are having a significant impact on the American political process.[40] That fact was further supported by the fact that Mike Pence was invited to address the 8000 delegates of the Southern Baptist Convention in 2018 to "express appreciation to Southern Baptists for the contributions we make to the moral fabric of our nation."[41]

Even more than Jimmy Carter, who was and is an ardent Baptist, or George W. Bush, who described himself as an evangelical whose favorite book is the Bible and whose favorite philosopher is Jesus, Mike Pence is the first legitimately conservative Christian to get this close to the American presidency. More than a few people I know have said they hope Donald Trump will not be impeached, because they would be greatly concerned about a Pence presidency and its impact on so many aspects of American social, political, and cultural life.

Would Moses Have Supported Pharaoh?

How do you preach about Seneca Falls, Selma, Stonewall, and Standing Rock at a time when the president of the United States has expressed little interest in empowering the people in any of those movements? His views about women are notorious (recall the *Access Hollywood* interview). His disregard for racial equity is apparent when he refers to neo-Nazi protesters as including "some very fine people,"[42] while referring to black athletes who protest police brutality by kneeling during the singing of the national anthem as "SOBs" who should be fired—because they are exercising a First Amendment right of free speech.[43] His abrupt announcement that transgender persons would no longer be allowed to serve in the military, done without consultation with the Pentagon, shows his lack of respect for the more than six thousand transgender persons currently risking their lives to defend this country as members of the armed forces. By authorizing the resumption of construction of the Dakota Keystone Pipelines he has revealed no interest in the expressed concerns of Native Americans either about sacred lands or about water and other environmental concerns.

It is interesting to note that Wes Allen's book offers its own set of themes that should challenge and inform preachers in the era of Trump. Allen lists race, gender, LGBT, and Islam or Islamophobia as his four categories. He and I line up perfectly except on the issue of Islam versus Standing Rock. However, I concede the legitimacy of his fourth point, and I trust he will do the same for me. As regards the issue of Islam, Trump has made his biases clear through his multiple attempts to impose a travel ban on persons coming from six predominantly Muslim countries and by his reckless re-tweeting to his millions of Twitter followers of a widely discredited video that claimed to show Muslims carrying out terrorist acts.[44]

The hypocrisy of his position is revealed in the fact that no terrorist act has ever been committed in the United States or against US interests in other parts of the world by any person coming from any of those six predominantly Muslim countries he targeted. Meanwhile, Saudi Arabia, which was the home country for the majority of the 9/11/2001 attackers, was not placed on Trump's list.

However, the main challenge for the context of preaching today is not Donald Trump as an individual, divisive and disruptive though he certainly has proven to be. The main challenge is the fact that 62,984,825 people in the United States voted for him, giving him a thirty-state win in the Electoral College.[45] Many of those persons are members of our churches and other communities of faith. They will be sitting in the pews every Sunday waiting to hear a word from the Lord. I remind you again of the model set forth by Cleophus LaRue.[46] You do not need to be Moses or Amos or John the Baptist every Sunday morning. Everyone seated in the pews will suffer the effects of death or sickness or some other personal tragedy. They will need guidance with personal spiritual formation. They will need to be challenged to support the ongoing work of their congregation and support the immediate problems of their local community.

However, the point about social justice remains important. As Wes Allen points out, speaking about social justice issues works best if we move from pastor to prophet.[47] He continues:

> **If we sound off as a prophet without our congregation (or members of it) knowing and trusting that we care for them, they will never accept us either as pastor or prophet. If, instead, we first establish a strong pastoral relationship with our congregation (and all its members), then they will trust us when we claim a prophetic voice, whether they agree with our stance or not.[48]**

Allen reinforces his point by talking about the pastor of the church in rural Alabama in which Allen would grow up many years later. In 1955 that pastor was urging his all-white, Methodist congregation to comply with the *Brown v. Board of Education* decision to desegregate public schools. Allen reports that the KKK harassed both the church and the pastor, and a swastika was once painted on the church door. Allen pointed out: "Some church members left, but most people stayed and supported Rev. Whitsett. I suspect that, to some degree, many sat in the pews with their arms folded and cotton balls in their ears, but they stayed. They stayed and tolerated Dan because he was their pastor before he was their prophet."[49]

This is good advice for those who would be preachers of the gospel in the context of twenty-first-century America. Preaching that moves between the role of pastor and prophet is part of the making of a preacher.

▪ ▪ ▪

Notes

1. Holly Meyer, "Convert to Condos or Remain As Is," *USA Today*, July 23, 2017, 1–2.
2. Ibid., 2.
3. Ibid.
4. See Rosalie Hall Hunt, *Bless God and Take Courage: The Judson History and Legacy* (Valley Forge, PA: Judson Press, 2006), which covers Adoniram and his three wives; Rosalie Hall Hunt, *The Extraordinary Story of Ann Hasseltine Judson: Life Beyond Boundaries* (Valley Forge, PA: Judson Press, 2018), which focuses on Ann's life and ministry with Adoniram.
5. Walter Fluker, *The Ground Has Shifted: The Future of the Black Church in Post-Racial America* (New York: New York University Press, 2016), 16.
6. Ibid., 27.
7. Eddie Glaude Jr., "The Black Church Is Dead," Huffpost.com, February 24, 2010, https://www.huffingtonpost.com/eddie-glaude-jr-phd/the-black-church-is-dead_b_473815.html.
8. Ibid.
9. Ibid.
10. Ibid.
11. Fluker, 224.
12. Marvin A. McMickle. This quote is engraved into a wall at The National Museum of African American History and Culture.
13. Joseph R. Washington, *Black Religion: The Negro and Christianity in the United States* (Boston: Beacon Press, 1964), 38, 44, 45.
14. Frank Thomas, *They Like to Never Quit Praisin' God* (Cleveland, OH: Pilgrim Press, 2013); Henry Mitchell, *Celebration and Experience in Preaching* (Nashville: Abingdon, 2008); and Cleophus LaRue, *Rethinking Celebration* (Louisville, KY: Westminster/John Knox, 2016).
15. Marvin A. McMickle, "An Epoch Event," in *Mr. President: Interfaith Perspectives on the Historic Presidency of Barack H. Obama*, ed. Darryl Sims and Barbara Williams-Skinner (Washington, DC: Salem Publishing, 2017), 61–62; cf. *The Audacity of Faith: Christian Leaders Reflect on the Election of Barack Obama*, ed. Marvin A. McMickle (Valley Forge, PA: Judson Press, 2009).
16. Rosie Gray, "Trump Defends White-Nationalist Protesters: 'Some Very Fine People on Both Sides,'" *The Atlantic*, August 15, 2017, https://www.theatlantic.com/politics/archive/2017/08/trump-defends-white-nationalist-protesters-some-very-fine-people-on-both-sides/537012/.

17. Eileen Sullivan, "Senator Insists Trump Used Vile and Racist Language," *The New York Times*, January 12, 2018, 1.

18. Emmanuel Akinwotu and Jina Moore, "How Trump's Comments Went Over with Africans," *The New York Times*, January 12, 2018, 1.

19. O. Wesley Allen Jr., *Preaching in the Era of Trump* (St. Louis, MO: Chalice Press, 2017), 7.

20. Ibid., 9.

21. Sarah Pulliam Bailey, "White Evangelicals Voted Overwhelmingly for Donald Trump, Exit Polls Show," *The Washington Post*, November 9, 2016, https://www.washingtonpost.com/news/acts-of-faith/wp/2016/11/09/exit-polls-show-white-evangelicals-voted-overwhelmingly-for-donald-trump/?utm_term=.1ebf1b5eae5f1.

22. Candace Smith, "Meet the Pastors Who Support Donald Trump," ABC News, April 14, 2016, https://abcnews.go.com/Politics/meet-pastors-support-donald-trump/story?id=38406350.

23. Daniel Lombroso and Yoni Appelbaum, "Hail Trump: White Nationalists Salute the President-Elect," *The Atlantic*, November 21, 2016, https://www.theatlantic.com/politics/archive/2016/11/richard-spencer-speech-npi/508379/.

24. Adam Cancryn, "David Duke: Trump Win a Great Victory for 'Our People,'" Politico, November 9, 2016, https://www.politico.com/story/2016/11/david-duke-trump-victory-2016-election-231072.

25. Marvin A. McMickle, "Church Leaders in the Wake of Scandals," *Democrat and Chronicle*, February 4, 2018, 37A.

26. Elizabeth Dias, "The Evangelical Fight to Win Back California," TheNewYorkTimes.com, May 27, 2018.

27. Amy Sullivan, "Democrats Are Christians, Too," TheNewYorkTimes.com, March 31, 2018. See also David Brody, "In Donald Trump, Evangelicals Have Found Their President," TheNewYorkTimes.com, February 24, 2018.

28. Michael O. Emerson and Christian Smith, *Divided by Faith: Evangelical Religion and the Problem of Race in America* (New York: Oxford University Press, 2000).

29. Michael Emerson, quoted in Campbell Robertson, "A Quiet Exodus: Why Black Worshipers Are Leaving White Evangelical Churches," TheNewYorkTimes.com, March 9, 2018.

30. James A. Sanders, *The Re-birth of a Born-Again Christian* (Eugene, OR: Cascade Books, 2017), 115.

31. Michelle Goldberg, "Donald Trump, the Religious Right's Trojan Horse," *The New York Times*, January 27, 2017, https://www.nytimes.com/2017/01/27/opinion/sunday/donald-trump-the-religious-rights-trojan-horse.html.

32. Ibid.

33. Ibid.

34. Ibid.

35. Ibid.

36. "Mike Pence Trumps His Boss on Religious Questions, but He Also Raises Some," *The Economist*, November 10, 2016, https://www.

economist.com/erasmus/2016/11/10/mike-pence-trumps-his-boss-on-religious-questions-but-he-also-raises-some.

37. Ibid.
38. Ibid.
39. Evan Halper, "He Once Said Mothers Do Not Belong in State Office. Now He Leads the Trump Cabinet in Bible Study," *Los Angeles Times*, August 3, 2017, http://www.latimes.com/politics/la-na-la-pol-trump-cabinet-pastor-20170803-story.html.
40. Sanders, 115.
41. Daniel Burke, "Southern Baptists Confront Painful Crisis," CNN.com, June 12, 2018.
42. Gray, *The Atlantic*, August 15, 2017.
43. Sophie Tatum, "Trump: NFL Owners Should Fire Players Who Protest the National Anthem," CNN, September 23, 2017, https://www.cnn.com/2017/09/22/politics/donald-trump-alabama-nfl/index.html.
44. Ashley Parker and John Wagner, "Trump Retweets Inflammatory and Unverified anti-Muslim Videos," *The Washington Post*, November 29, 2017, https://www.washingtonpost.com/news/post-politics/wp/2017/11/29/trump-retweets-inflammatory-and-unverified-anti-muslim-videos/?utm_term=.480f1aa0e332.
45. "Presidential Election Results 2016," CNN Politics, November 8, 2016, https://www.cnn.com/election/2016/results/president.
46. Cleophus LaRue, *The Heart of Black Preaching* (Louisville, KY: Westminster/John Knox, 2000), 21–25.
47. Allen, 26.
48. Allen, 26.
49. Allen, 26–27.

Chapter 9

Truth and Consequences

> Pharaoh said to Moses, "Get out of my sight! Make sure you do not appear before me again! The day you see my face again you will die." —Exodus 10:28, NIV

■ ■ ■

We now move to the fifth and final step in the making of a preacher: the consequences that could follow after a preacher delivers a sermon that boldly addresses issues such as have been identified in this book. If the only thing a preacher hears from a congregation week after week is how much they enjoyed the sermon, it is very likely that the preacher is not dealing with challenging content. There ought to be some sermons that, because of their content and the critique those sermons bring to the lives of the people in the congregation, might cause some people not to greet the preacher at the end of the service. There may be some sermons when a particularly disgruntled person gets up and walks out of the sanctuary due to the truthful but controversial nature of the content. Preachers are made when they experience some negative reactions to what they have said but find the courage to keep saying what the Lord has laid on their heart.

The question for this chapter is what are some of the consequences that might be directed to those who engage in *parrhesia* or bold speech? Remember that the term *parrhesia* has its origins with Socrates in Plato's *Apology*, when Socrates was forced to consume a poisonous drink (hemlock) because the people of Athens objected to his bold speech.[1] Socrates famously declared:

And this, O men of Athens, is the truth and the whole truth; I have concealed nothing, I have dissembled nothing. And yet I know that the plainness of my speech [*parrhesia*] makes them hate me, and what is their hatred but proof that I am speaking the truth? This is the occasion and reason of their slander of me, as you will find out either in this or in any future inquiry.[2]

It is not being suggested here that preachers are not effective unless and until they receive a death sentence for what they have said. What is being raised here, however, is the absolute certainty that if preachers today adopt the boldness of Moses as he confronted Pharaoh in delivering the message from God, there are some negative consequences that can be anticipated.

In *Be My Witness*, I make the case that a witness for the Lord is someone who sees something, has the courage to say something about what they have seen, and is prepared to suffer something because of what they have said.[3] The Greek word for witness is *marturia*, which is the basis for our English word *martyr*. Thus, in Acts 1:8 (NIV) when Jesus told his disciples to "be my witnesses in Jerusalem, and in all Judea and Samaria, and to the ends of the earth," he was urging them to be prepared for and to not run away from the possibility that what they preached might result in some negative consequences.

The July 28, 2017, edition of the *Peanuts* cartoon strip carried a significant message about the consequences that can follow when someone decides to preach on the topics being suggested in this book. Linus announces to Charlie Brown that he is "going to be a great prophet and speak profound truths." However, he tells Charlie Brown that he is quite certain that "no one will listen to me." When Charlie Brown says to Linus, "If you know ahead of time that no one is going to listen to you, why speak?" To which Linus responds, "We prophets are very stubborn!"[4]

Being Ignored Is the First Consequence of Preaching Like Moses

At the least, preachers who chose to address the themes mentioned in this book dealing with Seneca Falls (women's rights), Selma (racial justice), Stonewall (LGBT rights), and Standing Rock (the historic and continuing exploitation of Native Americans, coupled with the abuse of the environment) had better be just as stubborn as Linus has declared. That is because the first response to this kind of preaching is likely to be what Linus declared to Charlie Brown: "No one will listen to me." Angry responses, threats and intimidation, and tweets about your character and intelligence, such as frequently come from the current occupant of the White House, are not the first consequence that bold speech by preachers will generate. The first response is likely to be just what Linus said: "No one will listen to me."

The proof of that can be traced to the sequence of events that involved the destruction of the northern kingdom of Israel in 722 BCE and the destruction of the southern kingdom of Judah in 586 BCE. It cannot be said that the people of those two nations had not been warned that destruction was pending—destruction that was the result of their disobedience as covenant partners with Yahweh. In 750 BCE, more than twenty-five years before Israel was conquered by the Assyrians in 722 BCE, prophets like Amos, Micah, Hosea, and Isaiah had tried to warn the people and get them to change their ways. They tried to tell Israel that what God wanted was not the rituals and animal sacrifices that they were offering. Micah told them what God wanted when he boldly said:

> With what shall I come before the LORD
>   and bow down before the exalted God?
> Shall I come before him with burnt offerings,
>   with calves a year old?
> Will the Lord be pleased with thousands of rams,
>   with ten thousand rivers of oil?

Shall I offer my firstborn for my transgressions,
the fruit of my body for the sin of my soul?
He has shown you, O mortal, what is good.
And what does the LORD require of you?
To act justly and to love mercy
and to walk humbly with your God. (Micah 6:6-8, NIV)

Amos warned Israel with similar passion and clarity when he relayed the LORD's words:

"I hate, I despise your religious festivals;
your assemblies are a stench to me.
Even though you bring me burnt offerings and grain offerings,
I will not accept them.
Though you bring choice fellowship offerings,
I will have no regard for them.
Away with the noise of your songs!
I will not listen to the music of your harps.
But let justice roll on like a river,
righteousness like a never-failing stream!" (Amos 5:21-25, NIV)

The message of God could not have been preached with more clarity, conviction, or compassion. Despite such preaching around 750 BCE, Israel still was destroyed in 722 BCE. Why? Not because the people had not heard, and not because the prophets had not preached. It was because of what Linus told Charlie Brown, "I will speak profound truths, but no one will listen to me."

The same thing occurred with the southern kingdom of Judah prior to its destruction in 586 BCE. The prophet Habakkuk could not have been clearer when he spoke the word of the LORD:

"Look at the nations and watch—
and be utterly amazed.
For I am going to do something in your days
that you would not believe,

even if you were told.
I am raising up the Babylonians,
    that ruthless and impetuous people,
who sweep across the whole earth
    to seize dwellings not their own." (Habakkuk 1:5-6, NIV)

Zephaniah issued a warning when he repeated the word of the LORD:

"I will stretch out my hand against Judah
    and against all who live in Jerusalem.
I will destroy every remnant of Baal worship in this
place. . . .
    I will punish the officials
    and the king's sons
and all those clad in foreign clothes. . . .
At that time I will search Jerusalem with lamps
    and punish those who are complacent." (Zephaniah
        1:4,8,12, NIV)

Jeremiah was just as explicit about what awaited the people of Judah if they did not repent of their sins:

"I am about to summon all the peoples of the northern
        kingdoms," declares the LORD.
"Their kings will come and set up their thrones
    in the entrance of the gates of Jerusalem;
they will come against all her surrounding walls
    and against all the towns of Judah.
I will pronounce my judgments on my people
    because of their wickedness in forsaking me,
in burning incense to other gods
    and in worshiping what their hands have made. (Jeremiah
        1:15-16, NIV)

Ezekiel faced a similar situation when God told him:

Mortal, go to the house of Israel and speak my words
to them. . . . But the house of Israel will not listen to

you, for they are not willing to listen to me; because all
the house of Israel have a hard forehead and a stubborn
heart. See, I have made your face hard against their fac-
es, and your forehead hard against their foreheads . . .
do not fear them or be dismayed by their looks, for they
are a rebellious house . . . Mortal, all my words that I
shall speak to you receive in your heart and hear with
your ears; then go to the exiles, to your people, and
speak to them. Say to them, "Thus says the Lord GOD";
whether they hear or refuse to hear. (Ezekiel 3:4,7-11)

Those oracles were delivered at least fifteen to twenty
years before the fall of Jerusalem and the conquest of the
nation of Judah. A warning of what God was intending to
do was given. A reason for why God was about to act was
provided. A way to avoid that impending destruction was
offered. Nevertheless, as with Israel in 722 BCE, so Judah
was still destroyed in 586 BCE. Why? Not because they had
not heard the message, but because they did not listen to the
message that was so clearly delivered. The first consequence
of preaching on topics that challenge how people are living is
for the preacher to be ignored.

What Does It Mean to Hear?

One way to approach this issue of our sermons being ignored
by many who hear them is to consider the meaning of the Hebrew word *shema* as used in Deuteronomy 6:3-4 (NIV). Verse
3 says, "Hear, Israel, and be careful to obey so that it may go
well with you." Verse 4 follows by saying, "Hear, O Israel: The
LORD our God, the LORD is one." In this passage with its instructions about faithful living that follow in verses 5-19, hearing is not simply about audibly receiving the words that have
been spoken. Hearing is more precisely about acting upon the
words that have been spoken. Hearing does not really happen
with the ears if it does not cause someone to obey or act on the
instructions that have just been preached.

Hence, a preacher could easily be heard through auditory
speech, but never heard in terms of *shema*, as evidenced by the

fact that those who have heard the sermon do not and will not act on what has been delivered as the word of the Lord. That is exactly how things started with Moses when he went before Pharaoh. The first response from Pharaoh was to ignore Moses and dismiss what he had come to say. Things became more threatening as Moses persisted in his demand that the Hebrew people should be set free. But the first response to his message was to be ignored. As Linus told Charlie Brown, "I'll speak profound truths, but no one will listen to me." That is quite often the first response to our bold preaching.

Michael Eric Dyson employs this understanding of *shema* or hearing that results in some form of doing in *Tears We Cannot Stop*. He presents this book as a sermon to white people in America about the issue of race relations and white privilege. At the beginning of this fictional sermon he says, "I don't want to—really, I cannot afford to—give up on the possibility that white America can definitively, finally, hear from one black American preacher a plea, a cry, a sermon from my heart to yours."[5] Dyson was not interested in being heard in a merely auditory sense of the word. Dyson was hoping, or as he said, he was not ready to "give up on the possibility," that his words could result in some change of heart, or mind, or behavior on the part of white people in this country.

Sadly, many preachers and speakers for decades and centuries before Dyson had spoken on the same topics of race and white privilege, but their words were never heard in the sense that people acted in response to their words. From Frederick Douglass to Ida B. Wells Barnett to W. E. B. DuBois to Nannie Helen Burroughs to Martin Luther King Jr., there has been no shortage of the auditory sense of hearing. The problem for the last two hundred years or more, so far as the issue of race relations in the United States is concerned, has been a shortage of the kind of hearing that results in action on the part of the hearer: *shema*.

It did not have to take until 1920 for women to get the right to vote. Susan B. Anthony was calling attention to women's suffrage when she was arrested in Rochester, New York, in 1872 for attempting to vote. The first women's suffrage convention in Seneca Falls, New York, was held in 1848. That was seventy-two years before the Nineteenth Amendment to the US Constitution was adopted and ratified in 1920. Prior to that time, people were talking boldly on this subject, but most Americans were ignoring those calls for justice.

It did not have to take until 1865 for slavery to be abolished in this country. It did not have to take until 1870 for voting rights to be given to black males. It did not have to take until 1954 for segregation in public education to be deemed unconstitutional. Voices ranging from Frederick Douglass and Sojourner Truth to William Lloyd Garrison, Harriet Beecher Stowe, and Thaddeus Stevens had been boldly speaking against the evils of slavery, Jim Crow, segregation, white supremacy, and the terror that was employed by hate groups like the KKK to maintain a separate and unequal society. The civil rights movement of the 1950s and 1960s was not the first time the evils of racism in the United States were being addressed. That message extended as far back as the language of the Declaration of Independence and the framing of the United States when slavery was essentially ignored in the former and ratified at many points in the latter. The problem was not that earnest and committed persons were not speaking. The problem was that most people in the country were not listening.

In a stunning turn of events, when Donald Trump announced that transgender persons would no longer be allowed to serve in the US military, the leaders of all four service units (Army, Navy, Air Force, Marines) ignored his directive and publicly announced that they would not enforce what they believed to be an unfair and unjust policy. That is a far cry from how things were just fifty years ago. However, in other sectors of our society, including among many persons in many of our churches, there is a secret wish that the entire LGBT conversation would go back into the closet. People have heard the words, but they are not willing to act on what they have heard.

Standing Rock in 2016 was not the first time the issue of the rights of Native Americans and their concern about the preservation of the environment had been heard. The call for improved living conditions on reservations, the elimination of Native American images as mascots for sports teams, and the dangers to the environment through fracking and the construction of oil pipelines is decades old. The caricatured depiction of Native Americans in an endless stream of Hollywood films and television programs has been criticized repeatedly over the years. Native Americans have long objected to the use of images and logos such as the Cleveland Indians, the Kansas City Chiefs, the Chicago Blackhawks, the Florida State Seminoles, the Golden State Warriors, and the Washington Redskins. The issue is not that people have not heard the message. The issue is that people have heard but have not acted on what they heard. There has been no *"shema."*

Native Americans were attempting to be heard again during the 2018 US Open golf tournament. The tournament was held on a course in Southampton, New York, named Shinnecock. According to *USA Today*, members of the Shinnecock Nation were protesting the fact that the golf course was built over their ancestral burial grounds. They were also protesting the fact that the golf club "uses the image of an Indian wearing headwear as the logo for merchandise. . . . At the same time, the schools in Southampton do not include the history of the Shinnecock Indians."[6]

The issue of challenging people to hear the message on any of the themes discussed in this chapter is not the exegetical style or the sermon delivery techniques of the preacher. The issue is not the truthfulness or urgency of the message. There is nothing that can be taught in a homiletics class that can prevent a preacher from occasionally experiencing this first consequence of bold speech, which is to be ignored. This is a matter of understanding the biblical sense of "hearing."

Psalm 115:6 (NIV) says, "They have ears, but cannot hear, noses, but cannot smell."

Jeremiah 5:21 (NIV) says, "Hear this, you foolish and senseless people, who have eyes but do not see, who have ears but do not hear."

Ezekiel 12:2 says, "Mortal, you are living in the midst of a rebellious house, who have eyes to see but do not see, who have ears to hear but do not hear."

Matthew 7:26 (NIV) says, "But everyone who hears these words of mine and does not put them into practice is like a foolish man who built his house on sand."

Romans 2:13 (NIV) says, "For it is not those who hear the law who are righteous in God's sight, but it is those who obey the law who will be declared righteous."

Hebrews 3:15 (NIV) says, "Today, if you hear his voice, do not harden your hearts as you did in the rebellion."

Did We Really Hear Colin Kaepernick?

Much has been said about the decision by Colin Kaepernick, the quarterback of the San Francisco 49ers football team, to kneel rather than stand up during the playing of the national anthem before every game. One could ask the question of why the national anthem is played at all before every professional sports event in America. These are not political rallies or government-sponsored forums. These are highly partisan sporting events where, especially in the case of football, the players often engage in the most violent means possible to win the game. The singing of the national anthem does very little to create unity between fans and players, since fans regularly hurl epithets and insults, including the so-called N-word, at players on the opposing team. In Boston, the city that was at the center of the American Revolution, more than fifty fans were ejected from the game after "fans hurled racial slurs and a bag of peanuts at a visiting player." This occurred after a woman born in Kenya had just sung the national anthem.[7] I have written elsewhere about how little is the effect of the national anthem on the behavior of the players on the field or the fans in the stands.[8]

Kaepernick's decision to kneel during the national anthem was done to challenge players and fans alike to consider the contradiction between singing the national anthem and the continuing reality of racism in the United States. He said about his actions, "I love America. That's why I'm doing this.

I want to help make America better, and I think having these conversations helps everybody have a better understanding of where everybody else is coming from."[9] The writer of that article went on to say, "Unfortunately, far too many people didn't hear what he was saying."[10] Michael Eric Dyson captured Kaepernick's intentions in his own words. Dyson quoted this rationale for Kaepernick's actions:

> **I am going to continue to stand with the people that are being oppressed. To me, this is something that has to change, and when there's significant change—and I feel like the flag represents what it's supposed to represent, and this country is representing people the way it is supposed to— I'll stand.[11]**

Instead of being able to use his status as an African American who led his team into a Super Bowl in 2012, Kaepernick was viewed as being unpatriotic because he attempted to call attention to the issue of racism and discrimination in the United States of America. No less a person than the President of the United States decided to take time away from the failures of his party to produce a health care plan and from escalating tensions and threats of nuclear war with North Korea to comment on Colin Kaepernick and the other players involved in that form of silent protest. Under the guise of defending the flag and the troops, this four-time draft-deferred politician referred to those athletes in a speech in Alabama as "SOBs." It is clear that Donald Trump does not hear very well.

If Only People Had Heard the Message about Donald Trump

Trump had a very different tone when it came to the KKK, neo-Nazi, white supremacist rally that was held in Charlottesville, Virginia, on August 11-12, 2017. In his press conference on the August 12 Trump criticized the violence on "many sides." On August 15 he asserted that "there was violence on both sides," and that "there were very fine people on both sides."[12] Yet, only one side marched down the street carrying torches and shouting the 1930s Nazi slogan of "blood and soil." Only one side gathered in front of a Jewish synagogue, gave a Nazi salute, and shouted, "Seig Heil." Only one side was responsible for smashing a car into a group of counter-protesters, as a result of which a young woman was killed and many more were injured.

Trump's comments after the summit with North Korea's leader, Kim Jung Un, were just as shocking. When asked about human rights violations in North Korea that were not even mentioned in the June 12, 2018 summit between North Korea and the United States, Trump said, "I believe it's a rough situation over there. It's rough in a lot of places, by the way, not just there." That, despite the fact that Trump himself had earlier said in his State of the Union address that "North Korea has more brutally oppressed its people than any regime on earth."[13] This is a moment when the only way to explain our nation's present predicament is to invoke the word *shema*. All of Trump's Republican rivals in the presidential primary season of 2015–2016 and both Hillary Clinton and Barack Obama stated repeatedly that "Trump was temperamentally unfit to be President."[14] People heard their words, but they were not listening in the *shema* sense of the word.

Dr. John D. Gartner, who teaches psychiatry at Johns Hopkins University Medical School, says, "Donald Trump is dangerously mentally ill and temperamentally incapable of being president." He went on to say, "We have seen enough public behavior by Donald Trump now that we can make this diagnosis indisputably."[15] Nothing Donald Trump is saying or doing should come as a surprise to anyone in this country or around the world. Voters were provided with all this information and were clearly warned what the consequences could be if Donald Trump were to become president of the United States. However, even though the words were spoken, they were widely ignored by enough voters to provide Trump with a victory in the Electoral College even though he lost the popular vote by more than three million votes.

Here is another case where people heard but did not hear. As a result, our nation has suffered a significant loss of prestige on the international stage. That was reinforced a week after the events in Charlottesville when Trump responded to a terrorist attack in Barcelona, Spain. He invoked a long-debunked belief that General John Pershing told his soldiers to dip their bullets in pigs' blood and then ordered them to execute forty-nine Muslim insurgents in the Philippines during the Spanish-American War.[16] That was a claim that even the normally Trump-friendly Fox News debunked. This national embarrassment could have been avoided. However, whether it is preachers addressing congregations or discussions about national political elections, the risk is the same as the words of Linus to Charlie Brown: "I'll speak profound truths, but no one will listen to me."

The Second Consequence Could Be a Warning of Reprisals

If a preacher persists in speaking truths that listeners have attempted to ignore, the next level of consequences he or she may face can become more aggressive. It may take the shape of being told not to preach on a certain subject again "or else." The "or else" could be a stern rebuke, being reported to some ecclesiastical authority, not receiving a salary increase, or perhaps being removed from one's job or position. People may attempt for a while to ignore preaching that discomforts them. However, when a preacher becomes an annoyance or a nuisance or a troubler of the status quo, the consequences for such preaching can quickly become more threatening.

After several appearances before Pharaoh, the mood for Moses shifted from being ignored to being threatened. In Exodus 10:28, it becomes clear that Pharaoh had enough of the troubling preacher who was demanding freedom for the Hebrew people. He says to Moses, "Get out of my sight! Make sure you do not appear before me again. The day you see my face you will die" (NIV). Having one's preaching ignored is disheartening, but it is not a career- or even a life-threatening experience. When people who have some power over your life begin to threaten your livelihood, not to mention your life, the stakes for continuing with *parrhesia* or bold speech have been raised significantly. It is out of fear of having to face some reprisal that most preachers never say anything that could get them into trouble with anybody at any time. They have heard with their ears the words of Jesus in Matthew 16:25 that say, "For those who want to save their life will lose it, and those who lose their life for my sake will find it." The question is whether they are prepared to hear those words as a *shema* and put them into action.

Colin Kaepernick Faces Consequences for His Courage

Colin Kaepernick chose to kneel during the national anthem at the beginning of the football games in which he was about to participate as a star quarterback of the San Francisco 49ers. Rather than being heard in terms of the issue he was trying to raise, he has been punished for his bold stand by being released from the 49ers and not being signed to a contract by any other team in the National Football League. *Sports Illustrated* recently noted, "NFL team owners don't want to walk into their country clubs as the guy who signed Colin Kaepernick."[17] That is because of the message that Kaepernick is communicating. "His message is that we are flawed and we are failing our neediest people, and that's what scares people."[18] That is a message that many in this country, including the owners of NFL teams, do not want to hear, support, or be associated with in any way; especially if it could cost them a loss in revenue or fan support. So, Colin Kaepernick is a reminder that bold speech, even if it takes the form of a nonviolent, symbolic protest, can come with career-ending consequences.

Learning from Two Republican Senators

CNN recently interviewed two United States Senators, Lisa Murkowski of Alaska and Susan Collins of Maine. The interview focused on their decisions not to support the plan to repeal and replace the Affordable Care Act (Obamacare). They were the only two Republican senators who opposed the repeal/replace plan from the outset. The interview was less about their reasons for voting no and more about the pressure they felt to change their vote and some of the consequences they might likely face if they did not support the action that was being pushed by President Trump and by Senate Majority Leader Mitch McConnell of Kentucky.

Before the vote was taken in the Senate chamber they were both lobbied separately by Vice President Mike Pence, who serves as president pro tempore of the Senate, and whose vote broke a 50–50 tie that allowed the bill to be debated on the Senate floor. When all the Republican senators were invited to the White House to be lobbied by President Trump to gain unanimous Republican support for the bill, those two women were intentionally seated on either side of Trump at the table. Senator Murkowski was later threatened by Secretary of the Interior Ray Zinke with repercussions that would affect continued federal funding or projects in Alaska if she did not support the bill.[19]

After the vote was taken and both Collins and Murkowski voted no, criticism of their decision was swift and furious. Murkowski was the object of one of Donald Trump's infamous tweets. This one said: "Senator Lisa Murkowski of the Great State of Alaska really let the Republicans, and our country down, yesterday. Too bad!" Susan Collins was publicly denounced as being "dangerous" by Paul LePage, who is the governor of her home state of Maine. On the day before the vote, LePage criticized both Collins and Maine's other US Senator, Angus King (an independent who also voted no that day), saying that their refusal to support the bill was "disgusting."[20] It should not be overlooked that Senator John McCain cast the deciding vote against the bill. The difference was that he had voted yes to allow the bill to come up for debate and amendments on the Senate floor. Collins and Murkowski were steadfastly against the bill from start to finish.

During a CNN interview with Dana Bash, Collins and Murkowski were asked how they managed to withstand all the pressure they were under to change the way they were intending to vote. Murkowski spoke first, and her response was, "You cannot live in fear of the consequences of doing what you believe is right, whether those consequences come by way of the President, the Republican Party, or the leadership of the US Senate."[21] It may well be that Senator Murkowski was willing to ignore the pressure from Republican Party leaders because of her political history. She was reelected to the US Senate in 2010 without their support. She had lost the nomination of the party in the 2010 primary election because she would not do things their way. However, she won the general election as a write-in candidate over an opponent favored by the Tea Party movement and by Sarah Palin, the former governor of Alaska. Her bold speech and bold actions were not modified by fear of reprisals or consequences from those who disagreed with her words or her actions.

I refer to Susan Collins and Lisa Murkowski, not to take a position on the Affordable Care Act. I refer to them because they embody what this chapter is about—that saying and doing what you believe to be right often comes with negative consequences, criticism, threats, and intimidation. It can come with the possibility of future reprisals concerning your job security, your standing within certain professional or clergy circles, or your election or appointment to some position in a denominational structure that you might have hoped would come your way. Both of those female senators were willing and able to stand up to such pressures.

The question for the next chapter is the degree to which preachers are prepared to face negative consequences if and when they say something that does not meet with broad approval from their congregations. That is part of what is involved in the making of a preacher.

■ ■ ■

Notes

1. Plato, *Apology*, trans. Benjamin Jowett, classics.mit.edu/Plato/Apology, paragraph 11.
2. Ibid.
3. Marvin A. McMickle, *Be My Witness* (Valley Forge, PA: Judson Press, 2016).
4. Charles Schulz, "Peanuts," *Democrat and Chronicle*, July 28, 2017, C10.
5. Michael Eric Dyson, *Tears We Cannot Stop: A Sermon to White America* (New York: St. Martin's Press, 2019), 2017, 9.

6. Josh Peter, "Protesters Spread Word about Shinnecock Nation," *USA Today*, June 15, 2018, 3C.

7. Luis Gomez, "Fenway Park, Adam Jones and the N-Word: Red Sox Ban Baseball Fan for Life," *The San Diego Union-Tribune*, May 4, 2017, http://www.sandiegouniontribune.com/opinion/the-conversation/sd-red-sox-bans-baseball-fan-for-life-after-slur-20170504-htmlstory.html; Bob Nightengale, "Orioles' Adam Jones Berated by Racist Taunts at Fenway Park," *USA Today*, May 4, 2017, https://www.usatoday.com/story/sports/mlb/2017/05/01/orioles-adam-jones-berated-racist-taunts-fenway-park-peanuts/101187172/.

8. Marvin A. McMickle, "What Happens after We Sing the National Anthem?" *Democrat and Chronicle*, September 25, 2017, https://www.democratandchronicle.com/story/opinion/guest-column/2017/09/25/guest-essay-what-happens-after-we-sing-national-anthem/699234001/.

9. Paul Newberry, "We Need Kaepernick More Than Ever in Troubled Times," *Democrat and Chronicle*, August 19, 2017, 5D.

10. Ibid.

11. Colin Kaepernick, quoted in Dyson, 112.

12. Sam Levine, "Trump Called White Supremacists 'Very Fine People,' But an Athlete Who Protests Is 'A Son of a Bitch,'" HuffPost, September 23, 2017, https://www.huffingtonpost.com/entry/trump-colin-kaepernick_us_59c6846be4b0cdc77331a2f0.

13. Morgan Gstalter, "Trump on North Korea's Human Rights Violations: 'It's Rough in a Lot of Places,'" TheHill.com, June 12, 2018.

14. Susan Milligan, "Temperament Tantrum," *US News and World Report*, January 27, 2017, https://www.usnews.com/news/the-report/articles/2017-01-27/does-donald-trumps-personality-make-him-dangerous.

15. Ibid.

16. Alex Pappas, "Trump Cites Tale of Pershing's Pigs' Blood Bullets That Historians Dismiss," Fox News, August 17, 2017, http://www.foxnews.com/politics/2017/08/17/trump-cites-tale-gen-pershings-pigs-blood-bullets-that-historians-dismiss.html.

17. Michael Rosenberg, "Colin Kaepernick Can Be an Activist and a Football Player," *Sports Illustrated*, August 15, 2017, https://www.si.com/nfl/2017/08/15/colin-kaepernick-national-anthem-protests-charlottesville.

18. Ibid.

19. Bill Chappell, "After Trump Targets Murkowski, Interior Secretary Reportedly Warns Alaska's Senators," National Public Radio, July 27, 2017.

20. The Associated Press, "After Health Vote, Governor Calls Maine Senators 'Dangerous,'" ABC News, August 2, 2017, https://abcnews.go.com/amp/Health/wireStory/gop-gov-paul-lepage-maines-us-senators-dangerous-489885421.

21. Ashley Killough and Abigail Crutchfield, "Collins, Murkowski Take CNN Behind the Scenes of the Health Care Battle," CNN Politics, August 4, 2017, https://www.cnn.com/2017/08/04/politics/collins-murkowski-interview-cnntv/index.html.

Chapter 10

Truth Often Comes with Consequences

The LORD hardened the heart of Pharaoh king of Egypt, so that
he pursued the Israelites, who were marching out boldly.
—Exodus 14:8, NIV

■ ■ ■

There was a popular television game show that ran on
CBS from 1950 to 1954 and on NBC from 1954 to
1965 called "Truth or Consequences." The premise of
the game was that a contestant was given a few seconds
to answer some trivia question. If the question was not an-
swered correctly, then there would be consequences for the
contestant, usually in the form of having to perform some
silly stunt while on live nationwide television. During the
years when Bob Barker served as the host of that show, he
would end each program by saying, "Hoping all your consequences are happy ones."

As the story of Moses clearly reveals, the result of happy
consequences was not going to be the case for Moses after
he spoke the word of Yahweh to Pharaoh. When the people
of Israel left Egypt after 430 years of slavery, they had little
time to rejoice. Within a short period of time, they were being pursued by six hundred chariots of the army of Pharaoh
determined to return them to their former condition of servi-
tude. Suddenly, Moses was facing extreme criticism from his
own people. The consequences of their exodus from Egypt
did not appear to be happy. Trapped between the Red Sea

and the army of Pharaoh, the people seem to turn on Moses when they say, "Was it because there were no graves in Egypt that you brought us to the desert to die? What have you done to us by bringing us out of Egypt? Didn't we say to you in Egypt, 'Leave us alone; let us serve the Egyptians'? It would have been better for us to serve the Egyptians than to die in the desert!" (Exodus 14:11-12, NIV).

For purposes of this book, I would offer another angle to Bob Barker's closing refrain. I would say, "I hope preachers can remain hopeful and faithful when the consequences of your preaching could leave your listeners very unhappy, and who could then seek to make things very unhappy for the preacher."

It is not my intention to suggest that every sermon we preach should result in some form of censure or rebuke or criticism from inside the congregation or from somewhere in the broader community. Indeed, as has been stated earlier in this book, most of our sermons will necessarily address topics completely unrelated to matters of social justice. Recalling the categories of Cleophus LaRue, most of our sermons will involve matters of "personal piety, care of the soul, community concerns, and maintenance of the institutional church."[1] Pastors are not called upon to stand in the shoes of Moses, Deborah, Amos, Huldah, John the Baptist, or Mary Magdalene, who carried word of the resurrection to the Lord's skeptical disciples, every Sunday. If they do so, there will be a great many spiritual and personal needs in their congregation that will sadly go unaddressed.

However, there must come those times when LaRue's fifth category, social justice, must be at the center of the sermon. Sometimes a sermon must be preached that embraces matters that are controversial and unpopular with the listeners. Such a sermon is not always planned as part of a preacher's schedule of topics to be discussed. Often such a sermon is required in response to events that have unexpectedly occurred whether in the surrounding community or somewhere in the country or the world. I recall having my sermon planned for September 17, 2001. However, when the horrific events occurred on September 11, 2001, it would have been foolish and, frankly, unfaithful to have discussed any other topic the following Sunday.

Should preachers discuss stewardship on the Sunday after events such as the march and the murder that occurred in Charlottesville, Virginia, in August 2017? Should we focus on the benefits of daily prayer as a matter of spiritual formation on the Sunday after a jury acquitted police officers for the death of Philando Castile in suburban Minneapolis, Minnesota, even when the violence committed by those officers was caught on video and showed to the jury? Should we talk about the need to support the foreign mission efforts of our denomination on the Sunday after two people were killed in Portland, Oregon, while trying to defend two Muslim teenage girls who were being verbally assaulted on a commuter train by a white male passenger who was shouting he "wanted his country back"?[2] Righteous indignation is a valuable part of a preacher's spiritual makeup, and there must come those times when that side of a preacher comes blazing forth.

The question is why that side of most preachers is rarely, if ever, seen or heard. The theologian Reinhold Niebuhr may have the answer to that question. In *Leaves from the Notebook of a Tamed Cynic*, he says first, "I am not surprised that most prophets are itinerant. Critics of the church think we preachers are afraid to tell the truth, because we are economically dependent upon the people of our church."[3] His point here is how difficult many preachers find it to say anything that might upset or displease persons in the congregation whose financial support is essential for the work of the church and for the preacher's own salary. Loss of financial support is one consequence that many preachers may face when they speak boldly on some matter of social justice. However, Niebuhr offers a second rationale for an absence of bold speech from most when he says: "I think the real clue to the tameness of a preacher is the difficulty one finds in telling unpleasant truths to people one has learned to love. Thus, I'm not surprised that most budding prophets are tamed in time to become harmless parish priests."[4]

There is a third possibility regarding the silence of preachers when it comes to certain areas where one might expect
some moral outrage, and here again Reinhold Niebuhr
serves as an object lesson. In his book *The Cross and the
Lynching Tree,* James Cone takes aim at Reinhold Niebuhr
and all the white theologians of that same era of the 1940s
to 1960s, who were silent on the issue of racism, lynch mob
justice, and the repeated acts of terrorism against African
Americans by the Ku Klux Kan and other white supremacist
hate groups. They seemed to have a blind spot and an un-
willingness to use "parrhesia" or bold speech when it came
to issues of race. Cone described it this way, "Niebuhr had
the eyes to see black suffering, but he lacked the heart to feel
it as his own.[5]

Great Love Requires Bold Speech

The problem with refusing to speak boldly to the people we
love is that, sometimes, bold speech is the best way we can
demonstrate how much we love them and want the best for
them. Parents understand that part of the reason for disci-
plining a child who has misbehaved is because we love that
child and want the best for them. Failing to do so could well
result in allowing bad habits or attitudes to take root that
could lead that child into trouble later in life.

But is it really because we love the members of our congregation that we fail to speak firmly and adamantly about
the evils of racism, bigotry, and discrimination in which they
are either complicit or are content to remain silent? Or is
the reason because we are afraid of the consequences if we
say something that may offend them—a loss of their financial
support or our potential loss of a job? In other words, the real
reason why some preachers may not engage in bold speech is
not solely because of how their words might hurt or offend
their listeners but because of how the consequences of those
words might ultimately come back to cost the preacher more
than he or she wants to pay. Is the most loving thing to speak
boldly or to stand by silently? This calls to mind the words of
Martin Luther King Jr., who said:

> We will have to repent in this generation not merely for
> the hateful words and actions of the bad people, but for the
> appalling silence of the good people, . . . So often the co-
> temporary church is a weak, ineffectual voice with an un-
> certain sound. Far from being disturbed by the presence of
> the church, the power structure of the average community
> is consoled by the church's silent—and often even vocal—
> sanction of things as they are.[6]

The answer to that question will contribute greatly to the making of a preacher.

Writing in *Notes of a Native Son*, James Baldwin observed, "I love America more than any other country in this world, and exactly for this reason, I insist on the right to criticize her perpetually."[7] How much different life in this country might have been, could have been, and should have been if we had truly heard what James Baldwin was saying to America through his writings for more than two decades. His voice as a writer of books such as *The Fire Next Time*, *Go Tell It on the Mountain*, *Notes of a Native Son*, and *Nobody Knows My Name* were as important to the freedom struggle of the 1950s and 1960s as the sermons and speeches of Martin Luther King Jr. Sadly, neither of their voices was really heard.

Dr. King also linked his criticisms of America to his love for the country. Writing in "Letter from Birmingham Jail," King said:

> In deep disappointment, I have wept over the laxity of the
> church. But be assured that my tears have been tears of
> love. There can be no deep disappointment where there is
> not deep love. Yes, I love the church . . . But, oh! How we
> have blemished and scarred that body through social ne-
> glect and through fear of being nonconformists.[8]

Prophetic Critique Is Rooted in Divine Love

This idea of a prophetic critique being wrapped within the framework of a deep love for the object of that critique is

completely in line with biblical examples. The love that God
had for the nation of Israel was laid bare by the prophet Hosea
when God seems prepared to repent of the destruction promised throughout the earlier chapters of that book. Like a loving
husband who cannot give up on an unfaithful wife (Gomer),
God says, "How can I give you up, O Ephraim? How can I
hand you over, Israel? How can I make you like Zeboyim? My
heart has changed within me; all my compassion is aroused. I
will not carry out my fierce anger" (Hosea 11:8-9, NIV). The
fact that the destruction of Israel did occur in 722 BCE was not
a sign of the absence of love that God had for Israel. Rather, it
was what Dr. King defined as "deep disappointment" over the
laxity of the people in their obedience to God.

The entire ministry of Jesus is set within the context of
divine love. The act of incarnation was a manifestation of the
love of God for creation. That is the point of John 3:16-17
(NIV): "For God so loved the world that he gave his one and
only Son, that whoever believes in him shall not perish but
have eternal life. For God did not send his Son into the world
to condemn the world, but to save the world through him."

In Luke 19:41-44, there is a brief interlude between the
description of the triumphal entry of Jesus into Jerusalem
(Palm Sunday) and his going into the temple to drive out the
money-changers. The text says: "As he approached Jerusalem
and saw the city, he wept over it, and said, 'If you, even you,
had only known on this day what would bring you peace—
but now it is hidden from your eyes'" (vv. 41-42, NIV). As
Matthew records the same set of events, the love that Jesus
had for the people of Jerusalem was equally apparent even as
they were now on the receiving end of this prophetic critique.
He said in Matthew 23:37 (NIV): "Jerusalem, Jerusalem, you
who kill the prophets and stone those sent to you, how often I
have longed to gather your children together, as a hen gathers
her chicks under her wings, and you were not willing." This
language exudes a great love shrouded by an even greater
disappointment over the conduct and behavior of the people.
Of course, this passage also reminds us of the consequences
that can occur when someone tries to speak boldly to people

who are not willing to hear: "You who kill the prophets and stone those sent to you."

There is no way to disassociate the content of bold speech from the possible consequences that can affect the preacher of those words in ways that cannot always be anticipated. Preachers will never learn this lesson unless they speak boldly, as Moses did before Pharaoh, and run the risk of finding out about such consequences. What can be said about a preacher who has spent thirty or forty years in ministry, having preached between twelve hundred and fifteen hundred sermons, and has never faced any consequences, warnings, negative reactions, congregational rebukes, or even an anonymous letter that protested the content of a sermon? What has that preacher been saying all that time? Probably very little of any moral or ethical consequence!

So far as this book is concerned, so far as adopting the preaching of Moses as instructive of how we should—how we *must* shape our own preaching ministry, preachers must understand that bold speech about issues of justice and human equality will result in some consequences that will have to be faced. Such preaching is absolutely required if the church is to *be* "the salt of the earth" or "the light of the world" that Jesus has called us to be (Matthew 5:13-14). The only question that remains is whether preachers are prepared to face such consequences in their efforts to be faithful to God.

Remembering the Work of the Watchman

At this point, the words of Ezekiel 3 might be helpful as that prophet talks about the preacher as a watchman. He says:

> **The word of the LORD came to me: Mortal, I have made you a sentinel [watchman] for the house of Israel; whenever you hear a word from my mouth, you shall give them warning from me. If I say to the wicked, "You shall surely die," and you give them no warning, or speak to warn the wicked from their wicked way, in order to save their life, those wicked persons shall die for their iniquity; but their blood I will require at your hand. But if you warn the wicked, and**

they do not turn from their wickedness, or from their wick-
ed way, they shall die for their iniquity; but you will have
saved your life. (Ezekiel 3:16-17)

Ezekiel reminds us that preaching does not involve the
delivery of smooth, comforting words that serve only to re-
assure people that God is pleased with how they are living.
Preaching is the result of paying attention to what is going
on in the world around us and challenging listeners to heed
(hear) the warnings from God we are determined to deliver!

The "If" and "When" of Bold Preaching

The final issue to be considered here is "if" a preacher is ever
willing to say something about any controversial issue even if
there is biblical support for that position. More importantly,
is a preacher willing to speak on behalf of a point of view
that he or she already knows will not be well-received by the
congregation? It is hard to imagine that slavery, segregation,
or lynch mob justice against African Americans would have
lasted as long as they did "if" white preachers had been willing to speak out against such practices. Instead, churches are
still trying to find ways to deal with our nation's centuries-
long legacy of racism that is manifest in the fact that nine out
of ten churches in the United States are predominantly of one
racial group.[9]

Considering the content issues raised in this book (Seneca
Falls and women's rights; Selma and racial justice; Stonewall and LGBT rights; Standing Rock and honoring Native
American land rights), how much more quickly could those
issues have been resolved "if" all preachers of all races and
denominations and genders had been willing to speak out on
behalf of a just outcome for all involved?

Women would be welcomed into the ministry by local
churches "if" male preachers were willing to speak up and
support their efforts. The "Me Too Movement" that focuses
on the sexual abuse of women might have been unnecessary
"if" preachers had been more aggressive in dealing with issues of sexual abuse. That problem is front and center for

the Southern Baptist Convention as it deals with the failure of many of its leading preachers to take this issue more seriously.[10] A woman might have been elected President of the United States if so many voters in this country had not been willing to choose a highly flawed male candidate who boasted about his sexual abuse of women over a highly qualified woman.

It is quite likely that many voters cast their ballot for that male candidate based upon the invented doctrine of "complementarian theology" held by so many Southern Baptists. That view holds that while men and women are equal in the eyes of God, they are assigned by God to different, but complimentary roles in church and society.[11] "If" the 15 million Southern Baptists in this country were serious about changing their view about the role of women in church and society, then why does the 2018 annual convention in Dallas (which will attract more than 8,000 delegates) allocate only 12 minutes out of the 1,000 hours of the annual session for a woman to speak from the main stage?

The foolish accusation of the "birther" movement claiming that President Obama was not born in this country could have been stopped in its tracks "if" preachers of all racial groups had stood together and decried that obvious attempt to discredit this nation's first African American president. The shocking sight of neo-Nazis and members of the KKK carrying swastikas and Confederate flags down the streets of Charlottesville, Virginia, on August 12, 2017, could have been preempted "if" preachers in this country had spoken up loudly and clearly against the notion of white supremacy every time such groups sought to be heard. The blatant attempt to impose voter suppression techniques that would reduce the political influence of African Americans, among other groups, would have been abandoned long ago "if" more preachers were willing to speak against the racist logic that undergirds those efforts.

The hateful anti-gay slurs and attacks that are all too common in this country could be silenced "if" more preachers were willing to speak against such things rather than adding fuel to the fire through their own anti-gay bashing cloaked as sermons rooted in biblical truths. LGBT persons would be able to exercise their ministry gifts in our churches and would be able to enjoy the full range of rights afforded to every US citizen "if" more preachers had the courage to speak on behalf of those matters.

The continuing use of Native American images as logos and mascots for sports teams would be harder to sustain "if" people seated in the pews heard messages from the pulpit that challenged those customs and practices. Native American reservations would not be experiencing as much suffering as is presently concentrated in those places "if" preachers were to be careful to address that issue and those communities as deserving of the protections and opportunities for the pursuit of happiness that should be theirs as fully equal citizens and as children of God who "from one ancestor . . . made all nations" (Acts 17:26).

Moses Hid Behind "If"

The first step for Moses was "if" he was going to obey God's instructions to go before Pharaoh and demand freedom for the Hebrew people. Moses did not exactly jump at this call from God as a career opportunity. He offered one reason after another as to why he should not communicate God's message. There was a natural sense of humility with his phrase, "Who am I that I should go to Pharaoh and bring the Israelites out of Egypt?" (Exodus 3:11, NIV). That was followed by skepticism that the Hebrew people would not believe that God had sent him to achieve their liberation from slavery: "What if they do not believe me or listen to me and say, 'The LORD did not appear to you'?" (Exodus 4:1, NIV).

He told God about his inability to speak on any subject: "Pardon your servant, Lord. I have never been eloquent, neither in the past nor since you have spoken to your servant. I am slow of speech and tongue" (Exodus 4:10, NIV). Finally, Moses tried to refuse this assignment, saying to God, "Pardon your servant, Lord. Please send someone else" (Exodus 4:13, NIV). One could easily add another, unspoken hesitation on the part of Moses, namely, that he was a fugitive from Egyptian justice after having killed an Egyptian who was beating a Hebrew slave. All the above-mentioned hesitations could easily be driven by this preeminent concern—the likelihood of his own arrest and execution. The first challenge for Moses was "if" he was going to be courageous enough to say what God had commanded him to say.

"I Will Be with You": When the Preacher Speaks Boldly

The second issue that follows is reminding preachers to be prepared for the fallout and the pushback "when" a preacher finally decides to speak on a matter that is not likely to be well received but is exactly what that preacher believes God and Scripture are calling upon him or her to say. What was it that moved Moses from the "if" column to the "when" column? That is what I want to lift up for every preacher who is wondering whether bold speech might result in some negative consequences. Moses finally came to the awareness that God had made him a promise. God was not asking or expecting that Moses should be reliant on his own limited human strength or skill. God told Moses, "I will be with you" (Exodus 3:12, NIV).

In the case of Moses, the presence of God during his appearances before Pharaoh was embodied in the support he received from his brother, Aaron; in the power God had placed in the staff that had been given to Moses; and the physical displays of God's power both before Moses left Midian to go to Egypt and once he arrived at the court of Pharaoh. What gave Moses the courage to stand before the greatest political and military power on earth at that time was his confidence in God, whose power would eventually be proven to be too much for Pharaoh to match.

People can do extraordinary things when they are undergirded by these words: "I will be with you." I remember something as simple as the first time I was called upon to baptize persons by bodily immersion. I had never been trained to perform that ritual. I had taken no course that taught the techniques of lowering a person's whole body underwater and bringing them up again (alive). To make matters worse, this was set to happen at Abyssinian Baptist Church in New York City in front of twenty-five hundred worshippers. When I told the pastor, Dr. Samuel DeWitt Proctor, how worried I was about making a mistake during such a sacred moment, he offered me this great assurance: "McMickle, I am not going to send you in there alone. I am going in the pool with you." Sure enough, even though it was my hands that did the work that day, the comfort of having him with me in that baptismal pool gave me the confidence to proceed.

Two of the most important moments in the biblical story of salvation involved people who were prepared to proceed once they had received from God these reassuring words: "I will be with you." The first such moment came after the death of Moses, when God announced that Joshua was to be the one who would lead the Hebrew people into the Promised Land. First God said to Joshua, "As I was with Moses, so I will be with you, I will never leave you nor forsake you" (Joshua 1:5, NIV). Later in that same chapter, God reinforced that point by saying, "Have I not commanded you? Be strong and courageous. Do not be afraid; do not be discouraged, for the LORD your God will be with you wherever you go" (Joshua 1:9, NIV). As with Moses, the power and wisdom would not reside within Joshua. He would be empowered. He would be enlightened. He would be encouraged. What moved Israel in general and Joshua in particular from their prolonged grieving over the death of Moses to resume their journey to the Promised Land was this promise from God: "I will be with you."

A similar moment occurs in Matthew 28:19-20, when Jesus sent his disciples out to carry his message to the world. They were given a challenging assignment: "Therefore go and make disciples of all nations, baptizing them in the name of the Father and of the Son and of the Holy Spirit, and teaching them to obey everything I have commanded you" (NIV). It is not likely that any of them would have embraced that assignment had it not been accompanied by this promise from Jesus, "And surely I am with you always, to the very end of the age."

That was the promise given as an assurance to the first generation of preachers, and that same promise has been extended to every successive generation of preachers up to this present moment: "I will be with you." Add to those two moments in the story of salvation one timeless promise from God found in Psalm 23, a text that takes on special meaning in times of trial or testing, as well as in times of fear or uncertainty: "Even though I walk through the valley of the shadow of death, I will fear no evil, for you are with me" (Psalm 23:4, NIV).

Confidence that inspires courage. That is the final and the most essential step in the making of a preacher. As Jesus reminds us in John 15:5 (NIV), "I am the vine; you are the branches. If you remain in me and I in you, you will bear much fruit; apart from me you can do nothing."

The Promise of Divine Companionship

Let us now agree that one more word is needed if the making of a preacher is to be complete; that word is "companionship." Companionship with God through the Holy Spirit will sustain and encourage preachers as they seek to remain faithful to God. Under the best of circumstances, ministry is a challenging vocation. Whether one serves as a solo pastor or as part of a larger ministry team, there are moments when the weight and the worries of the job can bear down until they could eventually wear down the spirit of the preacher. That is the moment when we need to remember and then rest upon the promise, first given to Moses, that has been passed down to us.

A Message from Martin

This was the sentiment behind an experience in the life of Martin Luther King Jr. at his lowest moment during the 1955–1956 Montgomery bus boycott. His home had already been bombed while his wife and firstborn child were inside the house asleep. Vile and vicious threats on his life and the lives of his family were pouring in through phone calls at all hours of the day and night. In *Stride Toward Freedom*,

Dr. King describes his own father and others who were pleading with him to leave Montgomery and return to a secure position at his father's church in Atlanta, Georgia, or to Coretta Scott King's hometown of Marion, Alabama. The Kings decided to remain in Montgomery, but they were fearful of what dangers might still await them.[12]

Uncertain of what to do, Dr. King decided to "take my problem to God." He said to God:

> **I am here taking a stand for what I believe is right. But now I am afraid. The people are looking to me for leadership, and if I stand before them without strength and courage, they too will falter. I am at the end of my powers. I have nothing left. I've come to the point where I can't face it alone.[13]**

He then reports that the answer he needed came to him when he heard God say to him: "Stand up for righteousness, stand up for truth; and God will be at your side forever."[14]

Some years later, I heard Dr. King recount this experience from 1955. As he told the story to us in 1966, he added one more detail to the narrative. He said that as soon as he heard the reassurance of God's presence, the words of this hymn came rushing into his mind:

> *I've seen the lightning flashing, I've felt the thunder roll;*
> *I've felt sin's breakers dashing, trying to conquer my*
> *   soul.*
> *But I heard the voice of Jesus telling me still to fight on;*
> *He promised never to leave me, never to leave me alone.*
> *No, never alone. He promised never to leave me, never*
> *   to leave me alone.[15]*

Truth and Consequences in Chicago

My reference to the consequences that were experienced by Martin Luther King Jr. in his fight for civil rights in this country causes me to return to the year of 1966 when Dr. King came to my hometown of Chicago to launch an open housing campaign. Most of the African American population in that city, my family included, was clustered together on the city's south side in a section popularly called Bronzeville.[16] The objective of that campaign in Chicago was to demonstrate that racial segregation was not a problem limited to the American South. It was just as prevalent in terms of the neighborhoods in which people lived in northern cities as well.

Dr. King met unusual resistance to his presence in Chicago from two separate arenas of influence. His coming to Chicago was not well-received by Joseph H. Jackson, who was both the president of the National Baptist Convention and the pastor of Olivet Baptist Church in Chicago. Jackson leveraged all of his influence to deter other African American preachers from supporting the work of Dr. King.[17]

The other source of resistance came from the City of Chicago and especially its mayor, Richard J. Daley. Together, Jackson and Daley made sure that none of the major churches in town would open their doors for the community meetings that were a part of that 1966 summer campaign. The only notable exception to that closed-door policy was from Clay Evans at Fellowship Baptist Church. Along with Liberty Baptist Church, Fellowship was the only other major black Baptist church to host Dr. King. Liberty Baptist Church managed to avoid any known or announced reprisals for its willingness to stand with Dr. King. That was not the case for Clay Evans and Fellowship Baptist.

That congregation was in the midst of a massive building project that would involve a new worship center, administrative offices, and a community center. That project was funded by $500,000 in loans from some of Chicago's biggest banks since the church clearly had a large-enough membership and budget to support a large building loan. The groundbreaking for the new sanctuary began in the Fall of 1964, and by the summer of 1965 the steel frame of the church was already in place.[18]

After Clay Evans participated in a public demonstration against racial segregation in Chicago's housing patterns, "Evans was given an ultimatum. He was to withdraw his support of King, or his loan for construction would be stopped."[19]

Evans stood with Dr. King. As a result, "building permits were yanked. Banks rescinded and denied current and future loans to finance the project. The construction crews gathered their materials and drove their equipment and vehicles off the construction site. All that remained was the tall, steel skeleton frame of Fellowship's unfinished sanctuary.[20] Evans had been warned that the mayor could stop any structure in Chicago if he wanted. That was no idle threat. Clay Evans and the Fellowship Baptist Church found out the consequences of supporting Dr. King in a city that did not want or welcome his presence.

It would not be until December 1971 and with the help of Jesse Jackson, who had become a political force in Chicago, that banks along with various denominations and local churches pieced together enough funding to finish the construction of Fellowship Baptist Church that had been halted in the summer of 1966.[21] Evans believed that what he was doing was the correct thing to do, and that God would not abandon him or the church. He said about those seven long years between the halting and the completion of that building project:

> These days are to us what the wilderness was to the children of Israel. They will bring us closer to the Lord. We can and we will do for ourselves what we thought only other folk could do for us.[22]

There are consequences for those preachers who practice *"parrhesia"* or bold speech. But as it has been argued in this chapter, there is a promise that comes along with it, and that is the promise that God will be us when we stand up and speak out on God's behalf.

As God Was with Them So Will God Be with You

In describing the things involved in the making of a preacher, we have talked about the preacher's call to ministry and the assurance that grows over time that this is the work to which God has led and directed us. We have reflected on the preacher's character marked by past sins that God does not use to disqualify us from service. We have invited preachers to consider the content of their sermons that will regularly touch upon topics that grow out of such significant and controversial issues as Seneca Falls, Selma, Stonewall, and Standing Rock. We have reminded preachers that their words should be spoken both within and beyond the walls of a church sanctuary, and that their words must address the social and political contexts in which they and their listeners are residing. Finally, we have tried to prepare preachers to face the consequences that come their way when they preach sermons that might disturb the consciences or challenge the comfortable status quos in which some people happily exist. In short, we have invited twenty-first-century preachers to model their preaching through the prism of Moses as found in the book of Exodus.

Postscript in Honor of Dick Gregory

The comedian and civil rights activist Dick Gregory died just days before this manuscript was completed. In the obituary of this stellar figure in the struggle for human rights, this quote of his was included. It is a fitting way to end a book that invites people to engage in bold speech or *parrhesia*. Dick Gregory said, "If you put dirty clothes into a washing machine but take out the agitator, all you will have at the end of the cycle are wet, dirty clothes."[23]

If we want to make the world a better place, somebody is going to have to agitate! Preaching that results in agitation on issues of great urgency and importance will come more readily from those who embrace the five steps set forth in this book that contribute to the making of a preacher.

▪ ▪ ▪

Notes

1. Cleophus LaRue, *The Heart of Black Preaching* (Louisville, KY: West-minster/John Knox, 2000), 21–25.
2. "Suspect Named in Killing of 2 People Who Defended Muslim Women," CBS News, May 27, 2017, https://www.cbsnews.com/news/jeremy-joseph-christian-portland-stabbing-muslim-hate-speech/.

3. Reinhold Niebuhr, *Leaves from the Notebook of a Tamed Cynic* (Louisville, KY: Westminster/John Knox, 1957), 47.
4. Ibid.
5. James Cone, *The Cross and the Lynching Tree* (Maryknoll, NY: Orbis Books, 2012), 41.
6. Martin Luther King Jr., "Letter from a Birmingham Jail," in *Why We Can't Wait* (New York: Signet Books, 1964), 86, 91–92.
7. James Baldwin, *Notes of a Native Son* (New York: Beacon Press, 1955), 9.
8. King, "Letter from a Birmingham Jail," 91.
9. Mark Curnette, "Christian churches still struggle with race, how to discuss it, what to do" USAToday.com, June 12, 2018, https://www.usatoday.com/story/news/nation-now/2018/06/12/what-should-churches-say-do-racism/659935002/.
10. Daniel Burke, "Southern Baptists confront 'painful crisis,'" CNN.com, June 12, 2018, https://www.cnn.com/2018/06/11/us/southern-baptist-convention-scandals/index.html.
11. Ibid.
12. Martin Luther King Jr., *Stride Toward Freedom* (New York: Harper & Brothers, 1958), 115.
13. Ibid., 120.
14. Ibid.
15. Nolan Williams Jr., arranger, *African American Heritage Hymnal* (Chicago: GIA Publications, 2001), 310.
16. St. Clair Drake and Horace A. Cayton, *Black Metropolis* (Chicago: University of Chicago Press, 1945), 174, 383.
17. Sherman Roosevelt Tribble, *Images of a Preacher* (Nashville: Townsend Press, 1990), 104, 122.
18. Zach Mills, *The Last Blues Preacher: Reverend Clay Evans, Black Lives, and the Faith That Woke the Nation* (Minneapolis, MN: Fortress Press, 2018), 203.
19. Ibid.
20. Ibid., 203–204.
21. Ibid., 207.
22. Ibid.
23. Bryan Alexander, "Dick Gregory Shattered the Mold on Stage and Off," *USA Today*, August 21, 2017, 6B.

Bibliography for *The Making of a Preacher* and Other Recommended Readings

■ ■ ■

Achtemeier, Elizabeth. *Preaching from the Old Testament*. Louisville: Westminster/John Knox Press, 1989.

Alcantara, Jared E. *Learning from a Legend: What Gardner C. Taylor Can Teach Us about Preaching*. Eugene, OR: Cascade Books, 2016.

Allen, Donna E. *Toward a Womanist Homiletic*. Switzerland: Peter Lang Inc., International Academic Publishers, 2013.

Allen, O. Wesley. *Preaching and the Human Condition*. Nashville: Abingdon, 2016.

———. *Preaching in the Era of Trump*. St. Louis, MO: Chalice Press, 2017.

Anderson, Kurt. *Fantasyland*. New York: Random House, 2017.

Baldwin, James. *The Fire Next Time*. New York: Dell Books, 1963.

Barth, Karl. *The Preaching of the Gospel*. Philadelphia: Westminster Press, 1963.

Bond, Adam L. *I've Been Called: Now What?* Valley Forge, PA: Judson Press, 2012.

———. *The Imposing Preacher: Samuel DeWitt Proctor and Black Public Faith*. Minneapolis, MN: Fortress Press, 2013.

Brekus, Catherine A. *Strangers & Pilgrims: Female Preaching in America 1740–1845*. Chapel Hill, NC: University of North Carolina Press, 1998.

Brown, Teresa Fry. *Can a Sistah Get a Little Help?* Cleveland, OH: The Pilgrim Press, 2008.

———. *Weary Throats and New Songs*. Nashville: Abingdon, 2003. Brueggemann, Walter. *The Prophetic Imagination*. Philadelphia: Fortress Press, 1978.

Cannon, Katie. *Katie's Canon: Womanism and the Soul of the Black Community*. New York: Continuum, 2002.

Collier-Thomas, Bettye. *Daughters of Thunder: Black Women Preachers and Their Sermons*. San Francisco: Jossey-Bass, 1989.

Cone, James H. *Black Theology and Black Power*. New York: Seabury Press, 1969.

———. *A Black Theology of Liberation: Twentieth Anniversary Edition*. Maryknoll, NY: Orbis Books, 1986.

———. *The Cross and the Lynching Tree*. Maryknoll, NY: Orbis Books, 2012.

Fluker, Walter. *The Ground Has Shifted: The Future of the Black Church in Post-Racial America*. New York: New York University Press, 2016.

Forbes, James A. *The Holy Spirit and Preaching*. Nashville: Abingdon Press, 1989.

Francis, Leah Gunning. *Ferguson & Faith: Sparking Leadership & Awakening Community*. St. Louis, MO: Chalice Press, 2015.

George, Timothy, James Earl Massey, and Robert Smith, Jr., eds. *Our Sufficiency Is of God: Essays on Preaching in Honor of Gardner C. Taylor*. Macon, GA: Mercer University Press, 2010.

Gilbert, Kenyatta. *Exodus Preaching: Crafting Sermons about Justice and Hope*. Minneapolis, MN: Fortress Press, 2011.

———. *The Journey and Promise of African American Preaching*. Nashville: Abingdon, 2018.

Glaude, Eddie, Jr. *African American Religion: A Very Short Introduction*. New York: Oxford, 2014.

———. "The Black Church Is Dead", TheHuffingtonPost.com, August 23, 2012.

———. *Democracy in Black: How Race Still Enslaves the American Soul*. New York: Crown/Archetype, 2016.

———. *Exodus: Religion, Race, and Nation in Early Nineteenth-Century Black America*, Chicago: University of Chicago Press, 2000.

Griffen, Wendell. *The Fierce Urgency of Prophetic Hope*. Valley Forge, PA: Judson Press, 2017.

Harris, James Henry. *Preaching Liberation*. Minneapolis, MN: Fortress Press, 1995.

———. *The Word Made Plain: The Power and Promise of Preaching*, Minneapolis, MN: Fortress Press, 2004.

Higginbotham, Evelyn Brooks. *Righteous Discontent: The Women's Movement in the Black Baptist Church, 1880–1920*. Cambridge, MA: Harvard University Press, 1993.

Johnston, Graham. *Preaching to a Postmodern World: A Guide to Preaching to Twenty-First Century Listeners*. Grand Rapids, MI: Baker Books, 2001.

Johnston, Robert K. *Reel Spirituality: Theology and Film in Dialogue*. Grand Rapids, MI: Baker Books, 2000.

Kidwell, Clara Sue, Homer Noley, George E. "Tink" Tinker, *A Native American Theology*, Maryknoll, NY, Orbis, 2001.

King, Martin Luther, Jr. *Stride Toward Freedom: The Montgomery Story*. New York: Harper and Row, 1958.

———. *Where Do We Go from Here: Chaos or Community?* New York: Harper and Row, 1967. ———. *Why We Can't Wait*. New York: Signet Books, 1964.

Kysar, Robert and Joseph M. Webb. *Preaching to Postmoderns: New Perspectives for Proclaiming the Message*. Peabody, MA: Hendrickson Publishers, 2006.

LaRue, Cleophus J. *The Heart of Black Preaching*. Louisville, KY: Westminster/John Knox 2000.

———. *I Believe I'll Testify: The Art of African American Preaching*. Louisville, KY: Westminster/John Knox 2011.

———. *Rethinking Celebration: From Rhetoric to Praise in African American Preaching*. Louisville, KY: Westminster/John Knox Press, 2016.

McCracken, Robert. *The Making of the Sermon*. New York: Harper and Row, 1956.

McMickle, Marvin A. *An Encyclopedia of African American Christian Heritage*. Valley Forge, PA: Judson Press, 2002.

———. *A Time to Speak: How Black Pastors Can Respond to the HIV/AIDS Pandemic*, Cleveland, OH: The Pilgrim Press, 2008.

———. *Be My Witness: The Great Commission for Preachers*. Valley Forge, PA: Judson Press, 2016.

————. *Challenging Gender Discrimination in the Church*. Valley Forge, PA: ABCUSA Ministers Council, 2013.

————. *Let Justice Roll: Progressive Voices for Social Justice* (editor and contributor). Washington, DC: Progressive National Baptist Convention in partnership with Our Daily Bread.

————. *Living Water for Thirsty Souls: Unleashing the Power of Exegetical Preaching*. Valley Forge, PA: Judson Press, 2001.

————. *Preaching to the Black Middle Class: Words of Challenge, Words of Hope*. Valley Forge, PA: Judson Press, 2000.

————. *Pulpit & Politics: Separation of Church and State in the Black Church*. Valley Forge, PA: Judson Press, 2014.

————. *Shaping the Claim: Moving from Text to Sermon*. Minneapolis: Fortress Press, 2008.

————. *Where Have All the Prophets Gone? Reclaiming Prophetic Preaching in America*. Cleveland, OH: The Pilgrim Press, 2008.

Mills, Zach. *The Last Blues Preachers: Reverend Clay Evans, Black Lives, and the Faith That Woke the Nation*. Minneapolis, MN: Fortress Press, 2018.

Mitchell, Henry, *Celebration and Experience in Preaching*. Nashville: Abingdon, 2008.

————. *The Irresistible Urge to Preach*. Grand Rapids, MI: Eerdmans, 1991.

Moody, David L. *Political Melodies in the Pews: The Voice of the Black Christian Rapper in the Twenty-first Century Church*. New York: Lex- ington Books, 2012.

Moss, Otis, III. *Blue Note Preaching in a Post-Soul World*. Louisville: Westminster/John Knox, 2015.

Myers, William H. *God's Yes Was Louder Than My No*. Grand Rapids, MI: Eerdmans, 1994.

Niebuhr, H. Richard. *Christ and Culture*. New York: Harper and Row, 1951.

Niebuhr, Reinhold. *Leaves from the Notebook of a Tamed Cynic*. Louisville, KY: Westminster/John Knox Press, 1929.

Powery, Luke. *Dem Bones: Preaching, Death, and Hope*. Minneapolis: Fortress Press, 2012.

Proctor, Samuel D. *The Certain Sound of the Trumpet*. Valley Forge, PA: Judson Press, 1994.

————. *How Shall They Hear: Effective Preaching for Vital Faith*. Valley Forge, PA: Judson Press, 1992.

————. *Preaching About Crisis in the Community*. Philadelphia: Westminster, 1988.

————. *Samuel Proctor: My Moral Odyssey*. Valley Forge, PA: Judson Press, 1989.

————. *The Substance of Things Hoped For: A Memoir of African-American Faith*. Valley Forge, PA: Judson Press, 1995.

Proctor, Samuel D. and Gardner C. Taylor. *We Have This Ministry: The Heart of the Pastor's Vocation*. Valley Forge, PA: Judson Press, 1996.

Resner, Andre Jr. *Just Preaching: Prophetic Voices for Economic Justice*. St. Louis, MO: Chalice Press, 2003.

Riggs, Marcia Y, ed. *Can I Get a Witness: Prophetic Religious Voices of African American Women*. Maryknoll, NY: Orbis Books, 1997. Salvatore, Nick. *Singing in a Strange Land: C. L. Franklin, The Black Church, and the Transformation of America*. New York: Little, Brown and Co., 2005.

Sanders, James A. "The Betrayal of Evangelicalism," *The Bulletin of Colgate Rochester Crozer Divinity School*, Summer 2012.

————. *The Re-birth of a Born-Again Christian*, Eugene, OR: Cascade Books, 2017.

Smith, Christine A. *Beyond the Stained Glass Ceiling: Equipping and Encouraging Female Pastors*. Valley Forge, PA: Judson Press, 2013.

Smith, Christine Marie, *Preaching Justice: Ethnic and Cultural Perspectives*, Cleveland, OH: Pilgrim Press, 1998.

Stroud, Dean G., ed. *Preaching in Hitler's Shadow: Sermons of Resistance in the Third Reich*. Grand Rapids: MI: Eerdmans, 2013.

Taylor, Barbara Brown. *The Preaching Life*. Cambridge, MA: Cowley Publications, 1993.

Taylor, Gardner C. *How Shall They Preach: The Lyman Beecher Lectures and Five Lenten Sermons*. Elgin, IL: Progressive Baptist Publishing House, 1977.

Thomas, Frank. *How to Preach a Dangerous Sermon*, Nashville: Abingdon, 2018.

————. *Introduction to the Practice of African American Preaching*. Nashville: Abingdon, 2016.

————. *They Like to Never Quit Praisin' God: The Role of Celebration in Preaching*. Cleveland, OH: The Pilgrim Press, 2013.

Thurman, Howard. *With Head and Heart*. New York: Harcourt Brace and Company, 1979.

Tisdale, Lenora Tubbs. *Prophetic Preaching: A Pastoral Approach*. Louisville: Westminster/John Knox, 2010.

Titon, Jeff Todd. *Give Me This Mountain: Life, History and Selected Sermons of Reverend C. L. Franklin*. Chicago: University of Illinois Press, 1989.

Tinker, George E. "Tink", *American Indian Liberation: A Theology of Sovereignty*, Maryknoll, NY, 2008.

Tribble, Sherman Roosevelt. *Images of a Preacher: A Study of the Reverend Joseph Harrison Jackson*. Nashville: Townsend Press, 1990.

Trible, Phyllis. *Texts of Terror: Literary-Feminist Readings of Biblical Narratives*. Philadelphia, PA: Fortress Press, 1984.

Ward, James and Christine Ward. *Preaching from the Prophets*. Nashville: Abingdon, 1995.

Washington, Joseph R. *Black Religion: The Negro and Christianity in the United States*. Boston: Beacon Press, 1964.

West, Cornel. *Democracy Matters: Winning the Fight Against Imperialism*. New York: Penguin Press, 2014.

West, Cornel, ed. *The Radical King: Martin Luther King, Jr.,* Boston: Beacon Press, 2015.

West, Cornel with Christa Buschendorf. *Black Prophetic Fire*. Boston: Beacon Press, 2014.

Williams, Demetrius K. *An End to This Strife: The Politics of Gender in African American Churches*. Minneapolis, MN: Fortress Press, 2004.

Zink-Sawyer, Beverly. *From Preachers to Suffragists: Woman's Rights and Religious Conviction in the Lives of Three Nineteenth-Century American Clergywomen*. Louisville, KY: Westminster/John Knox Press, 2003.